To Possess a Dream

To Possess a Dream

John A. Ishee

BROADMAN PRESS, Nashville, Tennessee

© Copyright 1977 ● Broadman Press
All rights reserved.
4282-50 (BRP)
4252-53 (Trade)
ISBN: 0-8054-5253-2 (Trade)

Subject headings: CHRISTIAN LIFE // PSYCHOLOGY, APPLIED
Dewey Decimal Classification: 248.4
Library of Congress Catalog Card Number: 76-57507
Printed in the United States of America

To renew the hues in
a fading rainbow
To rekindle the flame of
desire that burns away
the dross and monotony
of life
To touch the center of life
and find again the source
of inner strength
To possess a dream as though
it possesses you
To GROW . . . knowing that
growing has its own rewards.

—John A. Ishee

Preface

Dreams mean different things to different people. So I feel compelled at the beginning to clarify the type of dream that this book is about. I am not concerned here with the dreams we have when we are asleep. I leave that to psychologists who have special interest in that subject.

Neither do I write about those unrealistic dreams that frequently are used as means of escaping the world of reality. Rather, I am concerned with a dream which is the essence of reality for Christians—the vision of growth and change within individuals who claim faith in Jesus Christ.

In recent years, books on personal growth and human potential have appeared in an unprecedented manner. Most of these books, while offering lots of practical help, omit what I believe to be the greatest resource for personal growth—the power that comes from personal religious faith.

This book is written for people who are concerned about growth in the Christian faith. I have drawn frequently from sources that are not distinctly Christian in nature, but I have sought to set the contributions from these sources within a Christian context.

My personal experiences are deeply embodied in this book. As John Bunyan wrote in *Pilgrim's Progress,* "I have sent you here enclosed a drop of honey that I have taken from the carcass of a lion (Judg. 14:5-9). I have eaten thereof myself also, and am much refreshed thereby.''

JOHN A. ISHEE

CONTENTS

Preface

1. Dreams: *Our Frame of Reference*   13

2. Esteem: *What Everybody Wants*   33

3. Belonging: *Risk and Reward*   49

4. Responsibility: *Blaming or Choosing*   67

5. Time: *Priorities and Practices*   83

6. Love: *Neighbors, Strangers, Enemies*   97

7. Witnessing: *Will and Skill*   107

Discussion Starters   119

Notes   122

Appendix   125

To Possess a Dream

Dream: A goal or purpose ardently sought.

Webster's Dictionary

The kingdom of God is within you.

Luke 17:21

And your young men shall see visions, and your old men shall dream dreams.

Acts 2:17

1
Dreams:
Our Frame of Reference

A fountain of hope erupting within . . . the ability to sit down with your own soul and be at peace . . . a sense of deep belonging with other people . . . the gratifying feeling of being in control of your life . . . using your time as a sacred gift . . . enriching your inner kingdom through learning to really love . . . and experiencing so much authentic joy that you must share it. These are some of the qualities you possess when you seek first the kingdom of God.

The kingdom of God was one of the topics that Jesus discussed the most. It is also the topic that most of us understand the least. "The time is fulfilled, and the kingdom of God is at hand" (Mark 1:15), were the words that Jesus used to inaugurate his ministry. He came to establish the kingdom of God on earth.

The kingdom of God has two dimensions. First, there is the *social* dimension. Jesus came to establish God's rulership in cultural and social relationships. He was world conscious. Jesus laid upon his followers the challenge of extending the kingdom of God into all the earth. In one century the course of human history was changed. The hostile powers of the Roman Empire crumbled under the challenge of the kingdom of God. The legalism of Judaism went into an eclipse as the love of

Christ showed through. The cold, rational movement of Greek mythology was aborted by the compassionate concern of the followers of Jesus. Of the early members of the kingdom it was said, "These [men] have turned the world upside down." (Acts 17:6).

Second, the kingdom of God has a *personal* dimension. The domain of the kingdom is the heart of the believer. "The kingdom of God is within you" (Luke 17:21), Jesus said. His teachings about the kingdom of God may be applied to the dimensions of the human heart as well as the entire world. In fact, the strategy for extending the kingdom consists of a person experiencing within himself its power and sharing it with others who have not experienced it.

My purpose is to explore the personal dimensions of the kingdom of God. What did Jesus mean when he said, "The kingdom of God is within you"? What is the nature of the inner kingdom? What is its potential? What obligations does it place upon the person who experiences it?

Dreams and Visions

"And in the last days it shall be, God declares, that I will pour out my spirit upon all flesh, . . . and your young men shall see visions, and your old men shall dream dreams" (Acts 2:17, RSV). The first members of the kingdom were possessed with hope of their potential. They sought to possess a dream—*the progressive realization of the kingdom of God within*. Through the eyes of faith they caught a vision of the kind of persons God wanted them to be and that they could become. They envisioned the dream that could become a reality—the dream of personal growth as they discovered a new power within them and a new potential before them.

Our dreams—that is, our hopes—far from being irrelevant and unsubstantial, are the foundation upon which we build for the future. To catch a vision of what we may become as Christians is the beginning point in Christian growth. When we fail to possess the dream of what it means to have the kingdom of God within us, we are destined to mediocre Christian experience. Calvin Coolidge spoke wisdom when he said, "Anytime you don't want anything, you get it."

We are incurable dreamers. The legend of Don Quixote and the story of Walter Mitty speak of man's incessant ability to dream about what he would like to become. Don Quixote is the story of a retired Spanish gentleman who, caught up in the romantic lore of knighthood, began imitating the lives of his heroes. He dressed himself in an ancient suit of armor inherited from his grandfather and, astride a bony old horse named Rosinante, set out on a series of knightly adventures. The henpecked hero of James Thurber's short story, *The Secret Life of Walter Mitty,* was a twentieth-century Quixote. In his imagination, he dreamed that he was a naval commander, a brilliant surgeon, the world's greatest pistol marksman, and a British bombardier. Such literary characters are exaggerations of real people. Their dreams were unrealistic. But their desire and ability to dream are characteristic of each of us.

> The fact is this: we all need a vision . . . because of the restless insistence of the mind to find answers to its questions and to organize reality into understandable patterns. A vision gives life predictability. My vision serves me as a frame of reference, a source of adjustment to reality. Because of my vision, . . . I know how to act.[1]

William Herbert Carruth has written in his poem "Dreamers

of Dreams'':

> We are all of us dreamers of dreams,
> On visions our childhood is fed;
> And the heart of a child is unhaunted, it seems,
> By the ghosts of dreams that are dead.
>
> From childhood to youth's but a span
> And the years of our life are soon sped;
> But a youth is no longer a youth, but a man,
> When the first of his dreams is dead.
>
> There's no sadder sight this side of the grave
> Than the shroud o'er a fond dream spread,
> And the heart should be stern and the eyes be brave
> To gaze on a dream that is dead.
>
> *   *   *   *   *
>
> He may live on by compact and plan
> When the fine bloom of living is shed,
> But God pity the little that's left of a man
> When the last of his dreams is dead.
>
> Let him show a brave face if he can,
> Let him woo fame or fortune instead,
> Yet there's not much to do but to bury a man
> When the last of his dreams is dead.[2]

In his memorable ''love'' chapter in 1 Corinthians, Paul stated that the three outstanding Christian virtues are faith, hope, and love. Our hopes—our dreams—are essential ingredients for claiming the abundant life that Jesus offers.

To say that we are dreamers says nothing about the nature of the dreams. There are good dreams and bad dreams. There are dreams that deceive and disillusion and there are dreams that fulfill.

In the American culture we have the "American dream," the vision of unlimited success within the reach, if not within the grasp, of every individual. I do not wish to discourage that dream. Too few people in the world have the opportunity to dream of victory over poverty and the experiencing of some measure of personal fulfillment. I do want to assert, though, that the pursuit of the American dream, if it is geared primarily to monetary success, does not guarantee a person feelings of wholeness, contentment, and fulfillment. It is quite possible that the furious pursuit of such dreams may lure a person into a style of living that prevents his giving attention to the values in life that can produce fulfillment.

As Richard Shelton has written, a person may "keep pushing this wheelbarrow of ambition down a bruised road toward blind decisions." [3]

In *Hope for the Flowers,* Trina Paulus wrote in a unique way about the thirst of people to climb the pillar of success. Her story is about Stripe, a caterpillar who reached beyond himself in search of meaningful goals for his life. Seeing all the other caterpillars traveling in the same direction, Stripe concluded that what they were doing must be right, so he decided to join them. He discovered that the caterpillars were competing with each other to reach the top of a "caterpillar pillar." He also learned that the caterpillars who reached the top were disillusioned when they discovered that the rewards for their efforts were insufficient to satisfy their longing for fulfillment. In time, Stripe realized that fulfillment in life comes from being transformed from a caterpillar to a butterfly.

To progressively realize the potential of the inner kingdom requires a transformation of our values. The transformation begins with a personal encounter with Christ. Through faith in

Jesus Christ the transforming dream begins to become a reality, as the believer progressively realizes the new power within him and the new potential before him.

Kingdom Characteristics

Much of what Jesus taught about the nature of the kingdom of God was spoken through parables and the Sermon on the Mount. An examination of these teachings provides insight into the characteristics of the kingdom person.

First, the inner kingdom is characterized by *a clarification of one's values*. Jesus stated that the kingdom of God is like a treasure hidden in a field which, when found by a man, prompted him to buy that field (Matt. 13:44). Overcome by joy and realizing its value, the man quickly took action to claim the field for himself. There was no ambivalence in his action. Furthermore, Jesus stated that the inner kingdom is like a pearl of great price that a man discovered. He sold everything he had to buy that pearl (Matt. 13:46-47).

I believe the main lesson of these parables relates to one's system of values. The farmer discovered the value of the field. The merchant knew the value of the pearl. Without hesitation, each sought to claim his discoveries, fully persuaded that their value was above the value of anything else. The basic question that Jesus confronts us with is, "Do we value the kingdom of God and its development within us above all the other objects and activities that compete for our attention?"

The values of the kingdom person were implicit in the life of Jesus. He was a personification of the value system that a Christian should possess. In addition, those values were explicit in his teachings, especially the Sermon on the Mount. (The skill exercises at the end of the chapter are designed to help you to focus on the values Jesus taught that we should hold as primary.)

Second, the inner kingdom is characterized by *growth*. "And he said, So is the kingdom of God, as if a man should cast seed into the ground; and should sleep, and rise night and day, and the seed should spring and grow up, he knoweth not how" (Mark 4:26-27). The focus of this parable is on the natural process of growth. It is natural for a planted seed to germinate and grow; it is natural for growth to occur in the inner kingdom. Jesus also emphasized growth in the inner kingdom with the following parables. "Unto what is the kingdom of God like? . . . It is like a grain of mustard seed, which a man took, and cast into his garden; and it grew, and waxed a great tree. . . . It is like leaven which a woman took and hid in three measures of meal, till the whole was leavened" (Luke 13:18-21).

When a person becomes a Christian, the kingdom of God is established with him. Through the work of the Holy Spirit, the kingdom of God becomes a reality in his life. At first, the inner kingdom does not influence his entire being. This in no way minimizes the impact of the initial encounter with God through Jesus Christ. It is, however, a way of emphasizing that a Christian must grow with his newfound faith. The initial experience of conversion is the entrance of the kingdom of God. A person must continue to have similar experiences that help the inner kingdom to permeate and influence each sphere of his life.

Third, the inner kingdom is characterized by the *willingness to use the gifts we have received from God*. In the parable of the talents (Matt. 25:14-30) Jesus taught that each kingdom person has talents or gifts. Those persons who use their gifts see them multiply and experience the affirmation of God. Persons who "bury" their gifts receive the stern rebuke of God.

The call to the kingdom is a call to risk: to make a commitment about how we are to use our gifts. Those people who are not willing to risk, who fear to venture, who want to "play it safe" experience very little of the progressive development of the inner kingdom.

Jesus calls us to be assertive in the use of our gifts and abilities. A current movement in the behavioral sciences is called assertiveness training. Assertion is a neutral term; it implies neither negative nor positive actions. To be assertive out of selfishness is inconsistent with the spirit and teachings of Jesus. But failures to be assertive in the use of our gifts and in witnessing to other people is equally to be avoided. Of the early disciples it is written, "When they saw the boldness . . . they took knowledge of them, that they had been with Jesus" (Acts 4:13).

Fourth, the inner kingdom is characterized by a *radical departure from old behavior patterns*. When it was appropriate, Jesus respected traditional Jewish customs. On other occasions, however, he not only departed from them but openly challenged their validity. His departure from customs was frequently confronted with the question "why?" "Why do you eat and drink with publicans and sinners?" (Luke 5:30). "Why do the disciples of John fast often, and make prayers, and likewise the disciples of the Pharisees, but thine eat and drink?" (v. 33). Such questions led Jesus to make the clear assertion that he did not come to repair an old religion; he came to call people back to true religion through faith. "And he spake also a parable unto them; No man putteth a piece of new garment upon an old. . . . And no man putteth new wine into old bottles'' (vv. 36-37).

The inner kingdom is not for the purpose of patching up an old life to make it better. *It is to create within us a new life.* ''Therefore if any man be in Christ, he is a new creature: old things are passed away; behold, all things are become new'' (2 Cor. 5:17). Old behavior patterns, old modes of thinking, and even old folklore religion are out of place when the kingdom of God enters our lives. The call of the inner kingdom is a call to give up our chains, to break the shackles of tradition that bind us and prevent us from experiencing abundant life.

> It is a strange and frightening discovery to find that the sacrificial life that Christianity is talking about is the giving up of our chains—to discover that what binds us is also what gives us a measure of feeling safe. . . . No wonder Jesus comments so often on people who look and look, but see nothing; and hear and hear, but do not understand. If we really saw and really heard, we might turn to him and become involved with a migrant people who may have no place to lay their heads when night comes.[4]

Fifth, the inner kingdom is characterized by *willingness to share our faith experiences with others*. Jesus said, ''The kingdom of heaven is like unto a net, that was cast into the sea, and gathered of every kind: Which, when it was full, they drew to shore, and sat down, and gathered the good into vessels, but cast the bad away'' (Matt. 13:47-48). Experiencing the kingdom of God within us is a call to share our experience with others as an encouragement for them to experience it also. We are to pray, ''Thy kingdom come'' (Matt. 6:10).

Kingdom people live with a clear sense of destiny, knowing

that God is the alpha and omega, the beginning and the end. At the eternal judgment, those who have not experienced the kingdom of God within them will be cast out into the darkness of eternity. What a vivid contrast between that harshness and what God really wants for each person. "The Lord . . . is longsuffering, . . . not willing that any should perish, but that all should come to repentance" (2 Pet. 3:9). The kingdom person shares his faith experiences out of two motives. First, he wishes that other people may share the joy of his relationship with God. Second, he is compelled by the love of God to help other people escape a dark eternity.

Finally, the inner kingdom is characterized by *joy*. When the Pharisees asked Jesus why he and the disciples did not fast, he answered, "Can you make the children of the bridechamber fast, while the bridegroom is with them?" Moses had commanded only one day of fasting—the Day of Atonement. The Jews had increased the practice of fasting until some could boast, "I fast twice in the week" (Luke 18:12). Religion for the Jews was stern and austere. Jesus brought joy to faith. He said that the kingdom of God is like a wedding, a time of joy. In contrast, Judaism was like a funeral. Judaism involved the burden and frustration of keeping endless rules. The kingdom of God is the joy of finding a buried treasure.

In summary, the inner kingdom challenges us to reexamine our values and through the use of our gifts to grow toward our potential. It is a call to joyful living within the realization that God is in control of our destiny. It is a call to a life of sharing, telling others about the personal meaning of the kingdom of God within. Such a life-style provides the resources for abundant living. No wonder Jesus advocated "Seek . . . first the kingdom of God and his righteousness" (Matt. 6:33).

A Kingdom Strategy

An ancient Roman coin was imprinted with the likeness of Janus, a Latin god with two faces. Perhaps the reason that coin existed was because it spoke of the nature of the people who made it. We possess one face that is symbolic of our Godlike qualities. The other face is symbolic of the dark side of our nature. Often we fear to look at either of these potentials in depth. We live between the two extremes, in the twilight zone of mediocrity in which we are aware of our mediocrity and afraid of our potential for both good and evil.

Elizabeth O'Conner in her book, *Our Many Selves,* reminds us of that which we all know—we're not one person but many. Each of us is darkness and light, love and hate, fear and courage, sadness and joy. A person in one of my workshops succinctly illustrated this point when he said, "One part of me wants to be a peacemaker; the other part of me wants to fight." Like the man Jesus encountered among the tombs, each of us is not one but many. We are legion. Our greatest temptation is the possibility of never doing badly or really well, but walking the tightrope between the two extremes. In such circumstances life is bearable but it is not joyous. We become that way when we deny our many selves, including both our pitfalls and our potential. Each of us possesses a dark side and a bright side. We begin the process of the progressive realization of the inner kingdom of God by exploring the full range of our being, by venturing out of the middle zone of mediocrity and coming to a greater understanding of both sides of our selves.

We often deny the dark side because we fear it. We fear the pain that may ensue as we open the doors to our dungeon of darkness. We would rather not look at it; we would rather keep the door closed. Actually, the door is never closed securely. The dragons in our dungeon have access to the outside. When we deny our dark side, we tend to bury our negative emotions. However, we do not bury our emotions dead. Rather, we bury them alive, and they live on to haunt us. Those live emotions buried within us often speak when they are not spoken to. At inappropriate times, they come out of the dungeon and express themselves in self-diminishing acts. And those buried emotions are often directed toward other persons. That which we deny in ourselves, we tend to project on other people.

The best way to be redeemed from the dark side is to acknowledge its existence. "If we say that we have no sin, we deceive ourselves, and the truth is not in us" (1 John 1:8). Second, we must confront our dark side; not to cherish it in an unchallenging fashion, but to make friends with it so that we can try to change. It is written of Saint Francis of Assisi that he got down off his horse and embraced a leper. Will I do the same for that dark part of myself that I suddenly met in a moment of insight? Or will I push that part of myself back into the dungeon of darkness, deceive myself into thinking that it does not exist, and suffer the consequences of that self's frequent haunting and destructive visits into the arena of my life where he is uninvited and unwelcome?

We may tend to fear not only the dark side of our being but also our potential. To live nobly calls for commitment. Often we live with the false notion that we can learn and grow without commitment. Thus, we let the dream about our potential die in the murk of mediocrity. The unfaithful servant of whom Jesus spoke in Matthew 25:14-30 was a person who was not willing to take the risk of using the talent that he had. He buried his talent and was an unprofitable servant.

Thomas Gray in his poem, "Elegy in a Country Church-yard," made the statement:

> Some mute inglorious Milton here may rest,
> Some Cromwell guiltless of his country's blood.

Gray was saying that many times there are people who live and die, never realizing any significant portion of their potential. If we are to realize the potential of the inner kingdom, we must use the gifts that God has given to us.

The New Testament is explicit in teaching that every person has received gifts from God. They are for the purpose of building up the body of Christ and for the work of ministry to other people. To neglect those gifts is to run the risk of losing them and never realizing the potential that God has placed within us.

Atrophy is a term used by medical science to describe the deterioration of unused parts of the body. Muscles that are unused tend to diminish in size and functional ability. Muscles that are properly exercised tend to be strengthened. Even so our gifts are strengthened or diminished, depending on the extent of their use.

A Kingdom Strategy

An analysis without some type of commitment can lead to a plaguing paralysis. If we project beyond ourselves to the setting of some personal goals that can help the inner kingdom to grow, we have taken the first step in a growth strategy. Personal goals are the building blocks for the dream. Incidental growth does occur as we live our lives every day. Sometimes circumstances pull us "screaming and kicking" into new arenas of life and we are forced to grow. However, the most consistent and effective means of growth comes through setting a deliberate course and sticking to it.

In Christian maturity workshops, I have found that people have a great deal of difficulty identifying personal growth goals in their Christian life. Therefore, I have identified several personal goals that seem worthwhile. These goals come from my dialogue with numerous people about the areas of their Christian life and influence that needs attention. These goals are illustrated at the end of the chapter along with other skill exercises.

The second part of the growth strategy involves the development of life skills. A national news network told the story of a man who received a strange wedding gift. When he was married in 1940, some close friends gave him an alligator from the swamps in Florida. The man moved to a New England state. It was necessary for him to build a large pool for the alligator to live in. As the years went by, the man began to discover that the alligator likely would live longer than the man. He also began to think about what might happen to the alligator when he died. He decided that the best thing to do would be to send the alligator back to the Florida swamp so that he could continue to live after the man died. However, the problem was not easily solved. Allie, the alligator, who for years had lived in a sheltered existence, was not prepared to live in the swamps of Florida. The National Forestry Commission, seeing his plight, decided to intervene and retrain the alligator so that he could survive in the Florida swamps. For several months, the alligator was progressively taught those skills essential to surviving within a new environment.

Goals that arise out of our dreams are very worthwhile. However, simply to set goals without seeking to acquire the skills essential to achieving them is to invite despair and failure. In the remaining chapters of this book, I wish to deal with some specific skills that I consider to be essential to the achievement of the dream that Jesus had for us.

Specifically, these skills are:

- How to develop and maintain self-esteem.
- How to establish intimate relationships with other people.
- How to become a responsible person.
- How to experience time in a positive manner.
- How to be motivated and guided in your actions by Christian love.
- How to share your Christian experiences in a comfortable manner.

Note that this book is divided into two types of activities. First, there are reading activities, the basic content presented in each chapter. Second, each reading activity is concluded with a series of skill exercises that you may carry out individually. The last pages of the book provide structure experiences for groups who wish to study the book.

* * * * *

Long before the coming of Jesus, the prophet Joel indicated that at his coming the old men would see visions and the young men would dream dreams. Peter, on the day of Pentecost, asserted that that had arrived. That day also arrives in the life of an individual when he confronts Jesus Christ in a personal way. Old patterns of behavior are challenged and a person is encouraged to dream about what he may become. He is encouraged to engage in the transforming dream—the progressive realization of what it means to have the kingdom of God within. It is a life directed toward ultimate values. It is a life of growth. It is a life of joy. It is a life of power. It is a life that like the pearl of great price, once discovered, is worth all that a person has. A person realizes that it is worthwhile to dispose of all that he has and seek first the kingdom of God. In the course of seeking first the kingdom, his other needs are met.

Skill Exercises

● *Clarify Your Dream*

1. Read the Sermon on the Mount from Matthew 5 to 7. As you read, keep a sheet of paper and a pencil handy. Write down the values that Jesus stated that his followers should possess.

2. When you have finished reading, write a brief paper in the first person that describes the Christian values that you wish to possess. "I want to be . . . " or "I have decided that I will . . . " are good ways to begin your paper. Be as definitive as possible as you compare and contrast your life with the teachings of Jesus.

● *Develop Personal Growth Goals*

1. Out of the previous exercise, determine some specific goals for your Christian life. Below are some personal growth goals that are important to many Christians. Look over the list. Add to the bottom any other goals that you think are important.

__To develop a greater degree of self-esteem or self-respect.

__To achieve a more satisfying relationship with my spouse.

__To achieve a more satisfying relationship with my children.

__To learn to listen more effectively to other persons.

__To overcome a personality characteristic that often hinders my relationships with other people.

__To overcome a habit that hinders my growth as a person.

—To learn to forgive people who offend me.

—To engage in a definite effort to continue my intellectual growth.

—To achieve a better relationship with my in-laws.

—To be more open and trusting in my relationships with people.

— To become more responsible for my actions rather than blaming other persons and circumstances.

—To become more tolerant of persons who differ with me.

—To become more aware of my feelings and deal with them in a responsible manner.

—To share more of my material resources with persons in need.

—To regularly engage in spiritual disciplines (prayer, Bible study, etc.).

—To better use my time for those things that I consider to be important.

—To share more of myself in the service of other people.

—To share my faith in a comfortable and spontaneous way.

—

—

2. Next, rate the goals in order of priority and list below the three that are most important to you.

   (1) _____

   _____

   (2) _____

   _____

   (3) _____

3. What are the obstacles which keep me from reaching these goals?

IN MYSELF	IN OTHERS OR THE WORLD
(1) _____	(1) _____
(2) _____	(2) _____
(3) _____	(3) _____

4. What can I do to eliminate or lessen the effect of any of these obstacles or shortcomings?

   (NOTE: You need not eliminate the block entirely. Anything you can do to lessen the force of the obstacle will start you moving towards your goal.)

OBSTACLES	WHAT CAN I DO ABOUT IT?
(1) _____	(1) _____
(2) _____	(2) _____
(3) _____	(3) _____

5. What are the next steps I must take to move me toward my goals?

   (1) _____

   (2) _____

   (3) _____

6. Who can help me achieve my goals?

WHO?	WHAT WILL I ASK OF THEM?
(1) _____	_____
	_____
	_____
(2) _____	_____
	_____
	_____
(3) _____	_____
	_____
	_____

Jesus said . . . Thou shalt love the Lord thy God with all thy heart, and with all thy soul, and with all thy mind. This is the first and great commandment. And the second is like unto it: Thou shalt love thy neighbour as thyself.

Matthew 22:37–39

One who does not love makes the other person wither and dry up. And one who does not allow himself to be loved dries up too. For love is a creative thing.

Helmut Thielicke
How the World Began

2
Esteem:
What Everybody Wants

His hand was trembling slightly as it reached out to shake mine. He was a young man in his early thirties, strong and handsome, but troubled. He was in Nashville on a business trip and called for an appointment. "I read your book, *From Here to Maturity,*" he said, "and I figured you were a person that would listen." I considered his words a compliment. I did listen. He told his story.

"You remember that part of your book where you state that a person should not wallow in unworthiness after he experiences the grace of God?"

I nodded yes.

"Well," he continued, "that's what I do most of the time: I am a Christian, but I seldom feel good about myself."

We talked for an hour or more about a problem that is not unique to this one person—the inability to maintain appropriate self-esteem.

The inner kingdom can be "a place called home." The progressive realization of the power and potential of the kingdom of God within us helps us to come to a positive assessment of the person who lives within the tabernacle of the skin.

The rabbis of Jesus' time had a favorite pastime of debating which of the commandments were the greatest. Accompanying

33

the debates was the expectation that when the Messiah came, he would be able to incisively identify the greatest commandment, thus putting an end to the argument. Jesus did not meet all the preconceived ideas of the rabbis, but he did, when asked, identify the greatest commandment.

> Then one of them, which was a lawyer, asked him a question, tempting him and saying, Master, which is the greatest commandment in the law?
> Jesus said unto him, Thou shalt love the Lord thy God with all thy heart, and with all thy soul, and with all thy mind. This is the first and great commandment. And the second is like unto it. Thou shalt love thy neighbor as thyself (Matt. 22:35-39).

We are to love others—as we love ourselves. Jesus recognized that self-esteem is a primary need. He did not discourage it. Rather he used it as the standard by which we are to measure our love for others.

What Everybody Wants

One of the special marks of man is that since the dawn of creation he has been a problem to himself. One way that he is distinguished from lower organisms is that he has more needs than other creatures. The needs drive him into a need-fulfilling quest. This quest has been given various names by writers and thinkers of past generations.

The quest for survival has frequently been identified as man's ultimate quest. There is validity to this assertion. Self-preservation is strong. But there is much evidence to indicate that it is not the primary motivational drive within us. People sometimes risk survival to reach goals they consider more precious than life itself. History is filled with records of many sensible people who have chosen to die in dignity rather than to live in shame.

The pursuit of pleasure has been identified as man's basic quest. Psychologist Sigmund Freud advocated that the experience of pleasure was the primary motive for man's actions. Obviously, pleasure is a strong motivation in our lives. But what about that countless number of people who forsake pleasure in favor of duty? The desire of the eye, the stomach, the ear, and the body can be satisfied, leaving us with the plaguing question: "Is that all there is to life?"

The desire for power is another strong force that motivates us. Psychiatrist Alfred Adler advocated that all of man's activities could be explained as the *will to power*. Admittedly, there is much evidence that the desire for power is strong, at least in some individuals. The indicting pages of history give evidence that man will kill his enemies, betray his friends, and even deceive himself, in his quest for power. There is also ample evidence to suggest that once the power-seeking person finally takes up residence in his power castle, he discovers that it is a lonely castle with fragile foundations. The achievement of power does not satisfy man's basic need; often it diminishes it. A feeling of power can easily be accompanied by a lack of dignity and self-respect.

The search for meaning has been identified as the basic driving force within us. During World War II, Victor Frankl experienced the injustices and pains of Nazi concentration camps. He was one of the minority of Jews who survived the devastating death blows of Nazi persecution. Out of his experience he wrote *Man's Search for Meaning* in which he advocated that the ability of a person to find meaning in life can be the primary motivational force. "If I know why,"

Frankl asserted, "I can survive any *how*."

Lack of meaning can result in a benign, mundane existence. However, the pursuit of meaning, *per se,* is like chasing a butterfly. The more you chase it, the more it eludes you. Once you quit chasing it and learn to live quietly with yourself, it lights softly upon your shoulder as a thing of beauty to be admired and cherished.

What, then, is the thing we want more than anything else? What is the pearl of great price or the treasure hidden in a field that merits our uncompromising efforts? It is self-esteem—the ability to love ourselves appropriately, to sit down with our own souls and be at peace. Robert H. Schuller, in *Self-Love: The Dynamic Force of Success,* has adequately summarized our primary need.

> I strongly suggest that self-love is the ultimate will of man—that what you really want more than anything else in the world is the awareness that you are a worthy person. It is the deepest of all currents that drive man onward, forward, and upward. All other drives—pleasure, power, love, meaning— are symptoms, expressions or attempts to fulfil that primal need for personal dignity.[1]

One's primary internal need is to experience self-esteem. When he experiences it, he is "at home" with himself. When he fails to experience it, he is like a person who lives in a haunted house. When self-esteem is gone, some people no longer want to survive. The absence of self-esteem robs us of pleasure. The ability to live powerfully diminishes and meaning eludes us.

The Language of Feelings

The dream of becoming—of striving to be all you as children of God must be—cannot happen if your life is spent in a self-depreciating manner. Self-depreciation is self-defeat. Appropriate self-love is power—power to love life, to love others—to love God. It is only when we have developed an appropriate and secure self-love that we can consciously deny our own needs to meet the needs of others.

None of us remembers how we felt when we were born. Nature does not allow us to penetrate the dark curtain of our memories and relive those feelings. Therefore, we have to philosophize about how it must have felt when we first started our pilgrimage called life.

John Locke, an eighteenth-century philosopher, advocated that at the time of birth each person was a *Tabula Rosa,* a blank tablet. Man at birth is neither good nor bad; he is potential—potential for good or evil, joy or sorrow, self-love or self-depreciation. If we are like blank tablets at birth, then our self-concepts are neutral.

We do not enter the world with feelings of low self-esteem. They are learned. We begin to learn them very early in our experience. When we enter the world from the mother's womb, the doctor lifts us by our fragile legs and gives us a solid whack across the posterior. Startled, we gulp the first breath of oxygen into our lungs. We cry because we have experienced a loss and have been hurt. We deal openly with our feelings; we don't bury them within us to gnaw at our feelings of self-worth. That's something we learn to do later! And the price we pay often is a feeling of low self-worth.

David Viscott, in *The Language of Feelings,* states:

> Our feelings are our sixth sense, the sense that interprets, arranges, directs, and summarizes the other five . . . Not to be aware of one's feelings, not to understand them or know how

to use them is worse than being blind, deaf, or paralyzed. . . .
The language of feeling is the means by which we relate with
ourselves, and if we cannot communicate with ourselves, we
simply cannot communicate with others.[2]

Each of us experiences feelings that have the potential of
robbing us of self-esteem. The less we are in tune with them,
the greater their effect upon us. Handling those feelings in a
constructive manner involves not disowning, denying, or sup-
pressing them, but acknowledging their presence within us and
choosing how we shall respond to them.

To feel is to be alive, even if the feelings are painful. To be
aware of those feelings helps us to deal with them. It is how we
respond to external events that determines how we feel, not the
events themselves.

Two feelings likely will surface when our esteem is
threatened. These feelings are guilt and anxiety. To restore
feelings of self-esteem, we must deal with these emotions.

Guilt results from the realization that we have violated a
moral, social, or ethical principle. Its consequences is a lower-
ing of self-esteem and a need to make retribution.

Guilt for the Christian may be classified in two categories.
First, there is authentic guilt that results from the transgression
of God's will. Such guilt, while a painful experience, if dealt
with appropriately leads us to experience God's forgiveness.

Confession of our sins to God is the appropriate way to deal
with such guilt. We can claim the promise that "If we confess
our sins, he [God] is faithful and just to forgive us our sins, and
to cleanse us from all unrighteousness" (1 John 1:9).

Every person experiences feelings of guilt because "all have
sinned, and come short of the glory of God" (Rom. 3:23).
People seek to deal with sin and its resulting guilt in different

ways.

Some people deal with sin and guilt by "psychologizing" it. They rationalize about their guilt feelings. Like the natural man described by David Head in his book *He Sent Leanness,* they pray, "We confess that we have lost all our ideals, but congratulate ourselves that we have reached that stage of maturity which makes it possible to live without such adolescent encumbrances." Such deception does not restore self-esteem; it diminishes it. When we deny guilt, we tend to bury it within us. Then we become the victims of unconscious guilt—guilt of which we are not aware. Unconscious guilt leads us to seek retribution for our sins through self-punishment. In other words, we take our sins upon ourselves, rather than confessing them to God and claiming the forgiveness that Christ offers.

Guilt from unforgiven sin leads not only to self-punishment but also to our projection of guilt upon others.

> We cannot stand the sight of our dark side, so we repress it, push it under, thinking we have thereby disposed of it. But we have not. We have simply pushed it into a place where it both has us in its grip and automatically projects itself on the person or nation we do not like; so the tension we will not stand in ourselves is carelessly and irresponsibly cast out to increase the tension and strife and anguish in our world.[3]

Thus, guilt leads us to engage in self-depreciation and self-punishment. Moreover, it influences our perception of other people. The person who is continuously hypercritical of other people may well ask, "Am I acting out unconscious feelings of guilt—guilt that I need to surface and confess to God?"

All guilt does not result from violation of God's will. At times it results from a violation of rules that have been imposed on us by authority figures—parents, teachers, and other people who have exerted influence over us. Such guilt is often referred to as *morbid* guilt. Morbid guilt results from adherence to rules that are neither good nor bad, merely customary. A graphic illustration was shared by Thomas Harris in *I'm OK/You're OK*. He told the story of a lady who always cut off both the hock and the butt of a ham before she placed it in the oven. When asked why she did it, she defended it by saying that it was the "right" way because her mother always cooked a ham that way. A few weeks later when visiting her mother she asked, "Why do you cut off both ends of the ham?" In her reply the mother explained that the ham was prepared that way because the oven was too small to accommodate a full-sized ham. Here is a classic case of how amoral customs have a tendency to become "right" things to do. That which is expedient for one generation often becomes "ethical" for the next. Such customs deserve to be examined to determine if they are worthy of preservation. If they are not, they deserve to be abandoned without feeling of guilt.

Anxiety is the fear of hurt and loss. The first experience of hurt and loss at birth is only one of many painful events *experienced in a similar nature,* that produces within all of us anxiety, a feeling of fear and dread. Unrecognized for what it is and uncontrolled in its effect, anxiety produces a compulsive, driven, restless person who possesses the chronic feeling that all is not well. Self-esteem is lessened as anxiety increases.

Anxiety is the fear that we cannot cope with what we imagine will happen. It is conditioned by past experiences and is projected into the future. But the effective approach to anxiety relates to what we do in the present. The best relief for anxiety is the experiencing of God's grace in our lives each day. I think that's what Jesus meant when he said, "Don't be anxious for your life . . ." (Matt. 6:25, RSV). Just as the manna from heaven was given daily to the Hebrews who wandered in the wilderness. God's grace is given to us daily. We cannot store it up or hoard it; we must receive a new supply each day. The only assurance we have about tomorrow is that Jesus Christ, who conquered death and is alive evermore, will be alive and available to give of his grace for tomorrow's problems. The only commitment that we can truly make is that just as we follow him today, we will follow him tomorrow.

God handles our anxieties in two ways. He may change the circumstances that contribute to our anxiety. One example is noteworthy. A few years ago my friend's wife became acutely ill. The doctor's initial diagnosis reported malignant cells in her one remaining kidney. She had lost the other one years previously in surgery. My friend left the hospital that day consumed with anxiety. "As I drove home," he said, "I prayed as I had never prayed before. It's unexplainable," he continued, "but a quiet peace settled over me. I knew that everything would be all right. The next day the doctor reported, in a mystified fashion, that further tests revealed there were no malignant cells." A miracle? Perhaps not, but one will never convince my friend otherwise. From his point of view, God intervened and performed a healing act in a very direct way.

I believe in miracles. If I did not, I could not believe in some of my prayers, because at times I pray that God will intervene in the natural course of events and make an exception. And sometimes God does just that.

Care must be taken, though, not to presume upon God. The

other way that God deals with our anxiety is to give us grace to cope with it. That is what Paul experienced with his "thorn in the flesh." He prayed for God to remove it. Instead, God gave him grace to bear it.

How does one deal with anxiety? First, he must recognize that he has it. Second, he must own it. That is, he must realize that it is his feeling; that he is responsible for it. Third, he must do what he can to relieve the source of anxiety, including asking for God's intervention to remove the causes. Finally, he must be ready to accept God's answer to prayer, whether the answer be the alteration of circumstances that cause the anxiety or the strengthening of the inner kingdom to help us bear anxiety with faith.

The Esteem Triangle

Self-esteem is never achieved in isolation. How we experience ourselves is inseparably related to how we experience other people and how we experience God.

To a great extent, we are the products of people who have loved us or failed to love us. Psychologists refer to this concept as social reinforcement. It works like this. When other people affirm our actions, those actions tend to recur with a great degree of frequency. When our actions are not affirmed, they tend to weaken and disappear. Therefore, if a person is not affirmed through love and acceptance, the expression of his personhood begins to diminish. Self-esteem weakens because of the lack of reinforcement. The popular song, "You're Nobody 'Til Somebody Loves You," captures a profound theological and psychological truth. How we belong to other people and how they belong to us deserves more than just mentioning. Chapter 3 is given to the need and skills of belonging.

Self-esteem is inseparably related to how we experience God in our lives. It is important that a Christian become acquainted with God as he is revealed in the Bible. Otherwise, he is destined to be captive to a concept of God based on the experiences of his past and the emotional and mental needs of the present. That is, he may create a concept of God out of his needs instead of yielding obedience to the God of the Bible.

God was in Jesus Christ. When we want to know what God is like, we get the true picture by examining the example and teaching of Jesus as revealed in the Bible. Furthermore, we experience the God of the Bible first-hand. In the process we discover as a personal reality that "If God be for us, who can be against us?" (Rom. 8:31).

> We read Scriptures and make our confession, and read Scripture and make our confession, and then one day something happens. We begin to see that we hold in our hands a Book that is a manual for change. . . . "Thou art my beloved Son; with thee I am well pleased (Matt. 3:17). When we, too, hear that voice . . . we shall no longer need a book that has a confirming title. That title will be written upon our hearts and there will be nothing that can keep us from preaching in towns and cities "You're OK, I'm OK." [4]

The esteem triangle is stated in the greatest commandments: Love God and your neighbor as yourself. The three are an intricate web that holds our experience of esteem together.

Act As If

Philosopher Herman Horne has reminded us that we live our way into patterns of thinking and feeling more frequently than we feel and think our way into patterns of living. His concept provides a key to maintaining self-esteem. In essence, it means that the person who wishes to maintain his self-esteem must begin to act in a way that allows himself to feel worthwhile. The following are several specific actions you can take to build and maintain your feelings of self-worth.

● Give yourself permission to love yourself. You are a child of God who loves you. Nothing can change that.

● Seek to fulfill your moral responsibilities, otherwise, feelings of guilt will diminish your self-esteem.

● When you have feeling of low self-esteem, own them and begin to deal with them. Don't indulge yourself in them.

● When you commit sin, confess it to God and turn from it. Claim God's grace and forgiveness.

● After you have asked God to forgive you, forgive yourself. Don't continue to punish yourself for the sins of the past.

● Seek the solace and comfort of people who love you. Be willing to accept the love they offer.

You are a new person in Christ. You can love yourself and not feel guilty about it. For many people, it is not easy, but God is our patient teacher. Sometimes it takes a lot of effort as is depicted in the following paraphrase of James Aggrey's "The Parable of the Eagle."

Once upon a time, while walking through the forest, a certain man found a young eagle. He took it home and put it in his barnyard where it soon learned to eat chicken feed and to behave as chickens behave.

One day, a naturalist who was passing by inquired of the owner why it was that an eagle, the king of all birds, should be confined to live in the barnyard with the chickens.

"Since I have given it chicken feed and trained it to be a

chicken, it has never learned to fly," replied the owner. "It behaves as chickens behave, so it is no longer an eagle."

"Still," insisted the naturalist, "it has the heart of an eagle and can surely be taught to fly."

After talking it over, the two men agreed to find out whether this was possible. Gently the naturalist took the eagle in his arms and said, "You belong in the sky and not to the earth. Stretch forth your wings and fly."

The eagle, however, was confused; he did not know who he was, and, seeing the chickens eating their food, he jumped down to be with them again.

Undismayed, on the following day the naturalist took the eagle up on the roof of the house and urged him again, saying, "You are an eagle. Stretch forth your wings and fly." But the eagle was afraid of his unknown self and world and jumped down once more for the chicken food.

On the third day the naturalist rose early and took the eagle out of the barnyard to a high mountain. There, he held the king of birds high above him and encouraged him again, saying, "You are an eagle. You belong to the sky as well as to the earth. Stretch forth your wings now and fly."

The eagle looked around, back toward the barnyard and up to the sky. Still he did not fly. Then the naturalist lifted him straight towards the sun and it happened that the eagle began to tremble and slowly he stretched his wings. At last, with a triumphant cry, he soared away into the heavens.

It may be that the eagle still remembers the chickens with nostalgia; it may even be that he occasionally revisits the barnyard. But as far as anyone knows, he has never returned to lead the life of a chicken. He was an eagle though he had been kept and tamed as a chicken.[5]

Skill Exercises

● *Examine Your Self-Esteem*

1. Write down those personality characteristics about yourself that you like the most. What do you consider to be your strengths? Remembering that we grow through magnifying our strengths, consider some ways you may develop your strengths more fully.

2. Now write down those characteristics about yourself that you consider in need of improvement. How do these characteristics hinder your self-esteem? Plan some definite actions to help you to overcome these hindering characteristics.

● *Get in Touch with Your Feelings*

1. What do you do when you experience guilt? Is it authentic guilt or morbid guilt? Develop a plan for dealing with guilt the next time you experience it.

2. What causes you to experience anxiety? Try replacing that anxiety with faith.

● *Strength Your Esteem Triangle*

1. As you read the next chapter, consider the people from whom you need positive social reinforcement. How can you relate to these people in a way that will enhance your self-esteem.

2. Write a one-page paper on "My View of God." Examine that view. From what sources did it originate? Is it consistent with biblical teachings? Do you experience God as being for you?

● *Act as If*

1. Name one strength that you wish you had or wish you

had to a greater degree._____
_____

2. What is the thing you do or say that is keeping you from using the strength mentioned in number 1? _____
_____

3. What are you doing when the thing you do or say in number 2 occurs?_____
_____
_____

   a. When does it occur?_____
   b. With whom? _____
   c. In what situation? _____

4. List three steps you can take to change the situation described above.

   _____
   _____
   _____

5. Rank the three steps in order of importance._____
   _____
   _____
   _____

6. Pray over them and begin to act to build your personal strengths.

We are, each of us, the product of those who have loved us . . . or refused to love.

John Powell
Why Am I Afraid to Love?

The man who will not accept the risk of loving and receiving love will live and die in emptiness.

Earl A. Looms, Jr.
The Self in Pilgrimage

3
Belonging:
Risk and Reward

There was a pall of loneliness in her eyes as she talked. "I know lots of people," she said, "but I don't know any of them very well. I seem to move from one world of relationships to another. I never know people for very long, and I never seem to know much about them. Why can't I establish any deep and lasting relationships?"

She seemed to feel that the problem was uniquely hers. But it wasn't. The matter of belonging to others and how we belong is the concern of all of us.

The kingdom of God within is always personal, but it is never private. It involves the giving and receiving of love and support from other people. "It is not good that the man should be alone" (Gen. 2:18) was the first commentary that God made about man after he created him. We cannot achieve the potential of the inner kingdom through private effort. The welfare of each individual is inseparably related to the support and affirmations of significant others. Emerson was right when he said, "Our chief aim in life is somebody who shall make us do what we can."

Crowded Streets—Lonely People

A huge clock in the Commerce Building in Washington

D. C. displays the increasing world population total. According to that clock, it took one million years for that population total to reach three billion. Then in only sixteen years it reached four billion people. And a total world population of five billion will be reached in a few years. It seems strange that anyone could be lonely in the world where there are so many people. Paradoxically, it seems that loneliness increases as the number of people increases.

Robert Hastings has provided a graphic illustration of the loneliness of our time. As the Christmas season grew near in 1969, a lady wrote a letter to the postmaster in Nashville, Tennessee. Enclosed was twenty-five cents in coin and a strange request. "Will someone in Nashville use this quarter to send me a Christmas card?" she wrote. The lady lived alone. She had never married and had no close relatives. For Christmas, she had asked that someone in a strange and distant city send her a Christmas card.

The factors contributing to increased loneliness are many. Increased mobility among people makes it difficult for them to stay in one location and "put down roots." Changing lifestyles in suburbia makes a sense of community difficult to attain. Fast paces and busy schedules cover our loneliness, but also contribute to it. When there is a pause, we discover that we live in haunted houses—houses occupied with the ghosts of loneliness.

Maybe you have experienced these feelings:

> People need people.
>> Why can't they say so?
> They need to clasp hands,
>> instead of crutches;
> People need to match answers,
>> instead of questions;

> They need love,
>> instead of reasons;
> People need to check their reflections
>> in someone elses's life-drenched eyes.
>> Why can't we say so? [1]

The need to belong is both instinctive and learned. We begin life with the basic instinct to relate to others. That instinct is nurtured, and the need to belong grows stronger as we mature. Unfortunately, our skills in belonging do not always keep pace with our need to belong. W. W. Broadbent describes our dilemma as follows:

> Everyone wants to belong, but many people just don't know how to go about it. The hard fact is that some of us seem to experience much belonging and others very little. Some of us are very accepted by most people, and others aren't. Some seem to find an ongoing permanent love, and others stumble out of one alleged love experience into another. [2]

Every person needs love and acceptance from others. William Glasser in *Reality Therapy* states that every person needs at least one other person who loves him and accepts him if he is to meet his emotional needs. The paradox is this: If we seek to make people love us we usually drive them away from us. Some people, in an effort to get people to love them, become notorious love-seekers. They become what C. S. Lewis, in his book, *Four Loves,* calls ". . . those pathetic people who simply want friends and can never make any."

Levels of Belonging

The inner kingdom compels us to love people, but intimacy, a close relationship with people in which we share life on a deep level, is not possible with all people. To seek intimacy with all people may result in not achieving a close relationship with anyone.

We can learn a lot from the example of Jesus. He loved the whole world. It was for every person that he carried out his redemptive mission. But a close positive relationship with all people was not possible. For example, he was never able to establish a positive relationship with the Pharisees and Sadducees.

Furthermore, among those people who responded positively to his life and teachings, there were levels of relationships. Many people followed Jesus, but from his many followers, "He chose twelve, who also he named apostles" (Luke 6:13). Of these twelve, only three shared the joys of the transfiguration and the agony of Gethsemane.

Our interpersonal relationships may be classified into four categories. First, we must face the unfortunate fact that with some people we will probably never develop positive relationships. We should be cautious, though, to assure that we do not relinquish our Christian responsibility toward such people. Paul reminds us, "If it be possible, as much as lieth in you, live peaceably with all men" (Rom. 12:18). In effect, Paul advocated that to the extent that a peaceful relationship depends on us, we should try to relate positively to all people. His admonition is not a call to abandon "difficult" people. Rather, it is a reminder to fulfill our responsibility of continuing to exemplify Christian behavior in their presence.

Second, the inner kingdom calls us to a loving concern for all people. Christians are compelled to nourish a genuine desire to help the human race as if they were all members of one family.

Following the death of F. Scott Fitzgerald, there was found among his private papers a list of themes from which he intended to some day write short stories. One of them, read, ''Suggestion for a story—A widely separated family inherits a house in which they have to live together.'' The idea was not original with Fitzgerald. We have inherited a house from God—the world. All the people must live in it. The best hope of living together is within the love relationship that Jesus exemplified and taught.

Third, each of us has his own world of relationships, the network of people with whom we come in contact in the normal course of daily activities. The levels of relationships vary among the people of one's unique world. It is within this world that we have the opportunity to either enhance or diminish our Christian witness and influence.

Finally, each person needs a world of intimate relationships. The people in the intimate world of relationships are the ones we can trust the most, the people with whom we can share life. They know us for who we are, both our strengths and weaknesses, and accept us—often not because of them, but in spite of them. The love relationship between people in the intimate world is exceeded only by God's love for us.

For some people the intimate world is practically nonexistent. For others it is painfully small. *The extent that we can enlarge the intimate world affects our feeling of belonging and diminishes our feelings of loneliness.*

Semi-Belonging: Obstacles to Intimacy

Intimate belonging is often frustrated because we choose to belong on less authentic and more superficial levels. Efforts to belong often lead people to adopt semi-belonging styles. A semi-belonging style is an attempt to manipulate another person for love and approval. In semi-belonging, we play games in attempts to gouge from someone else some type of affirmation. The results, rather than being the development of love relationships, often are just the opposite. We either drive people away from us or the relationship settles into a level of semi-belonging where intimacy does not exist.

One semi-belonging style is self-depreciation. Unworthiness is often paraded as a virtue. Often, it is an effort to extract from others some type of approval. Ironically, the person operates on the false assumption that if he depreciates himself, it will result in appreciation from others. In effect, he says, "Look how unworthy I am. Don't you love me for it?"

The self-depreciating person may leave the impression that he is not worthy of being appreciated. Moreover, through his self-depreciating game, he pretends to reject the expressions of appreciation offered by other people. Their expressions of appreciation are not reinforced. Consequently, they become extinct.

Take Mary, for example. Mary is a very talented person. She is a leader in her community, giving much of her time to charitable projects. After a successful fund-raising campaign for a new library, Mary's friends compliment her for a job well done. She shrugs the compliments by saying, "Anybody could have done it," or "We were just lucky." Is Mary sincere? Or is she subtly manipulating her friends for even more love and acceptance than they are already offering? Probably, it is the latter. Would not the acceptance of a well-deserved compliment achieve the task better?

Another semi-belonging style is the "shiny halo" syndrome. Goodness is used as a way to buy belonging. The "shiny halo" syndrome affects people in religious as well as nonreligious circles, but people who are heavily involved in church activities seem to be more susceptible to its influence.

The inner kingdom places upon us a high ethical standard. Make no mistake about that. The call to follow Jesus is a call to moral responsibility. The danger, however, is that while maintaining noble ethical standards, we may become judgmental of other people whose values differ from ours. We may become like the Pharisee of whom Jesus spoke in Luke 18:11-12. "The Pharisee stood and prayed thus with himself, God, I thank thee, that I am not as other men are, extortioners, unjust, adulterers . . . I fast twice in a week, I give tithes of all that I possess."

The person with the shiny halo usually pushes other people away from him. They know he is human, that he has his scruples and shortcomings like other people. They also sense that he is not honest enough with himself and other people to admit them. They have the notion that if they share intimately with him, they will receive more judgment than mercy. Consequently, they maintain a safe distance. People share their deep secrets only with people whom they feel they can trust, people who will hear them rather than judge them. But the person with a shiny halo often radiates a judgmental attitude. Therefore, intimacy with other people is seldom possible. Even in the presence of other people who seek to keep their halos shiny, trust is difficult. Belonging between shiny halo people is very much like the fisherman who commented to his partner, "All fishermen are liars 'cept me and you. And . . . sometimes . . . sometimes, Joe, I ain't so sure about you."

Another semi-belonging style is flexibility born of fear. We become what other people want us to become or imply that we agree with people when we do not as a means of gaining acceptance and belonging. We become like the chameleon who changes his color to blend in with his environment.

Admittedly, flexibility is a good quality in our changing world. Like Jesus, we often need to examine traditions and access their validity. But when we adopt a flexible life-style born out of the fear of nonacceptance, we sacrifice integrity.

Integrity means wholeness. The word comes from the mathematical term *integer,* which is a number that isn't divided. A person of integrity isn't divided against himself. He doesn't think one thing and say another. He doesn't believe one thing and do another. He is not in conflict with his own principles. Integrity is the absence of inner warfare, which enhances one's ability to act consistently. When integrity is absent, there is division in the inner kingdom. Jesus said, "If a house be divided against itself, that house cannot stand" (Mark 3:25).

Flexibility born of fear diminishes our ability to establish our identity. The absence of internalized rules and principles to guide us can result in our being so expedient that we really do not know who we are or what we stand for. Consequently, it is difficult for us to develop deeper belonging with other people because they are never certain what type of person they are trying to belong to.

Another semi-belonging style is martyrdom. The martyr often reminds people of how he sacrifices for others. These reminders are given in an effort to win the acceptance of others. Does it work? Usually, no. The martyr seeks to induce guilt in the other person. The result is either abandonment of the relationship or the development of a relationship based not on love, but on appeasement.

L. O. Griffith, a Baptist minister, spent most of his adult life in Appalachia ministering to the needs of mountain people. Frequently, his friends would comment to him about the sacrifices he had made in order to carry out his ministry. "My 'sacrifices,' " he would reply, "meant giving up half-interest in a thirty-five acre, rocky hillside farm and in a one-eyed mule." No wonder he was loved and accepted by the mountain people. He refused to play the martyr role.

A final semi-belonging style that I will mention is the "guru complex." The guru complex is an attempt to appear all wise and all sufficient. Intellectualism becomes a facade behind which the self may hide. The guru has all the answers. He spins theories with ease and gives advice freely. But other people seldom know who he is—really.

The guru diminishes other people by trying to take responsibility for them. The relationship that usually develops is a parent-child relationship. If people follow his advice, they often feel less than human. If they do not follow his advice, the relationship is usually abandoned.

Semi-belonging styles are numerous. Basically, they are characterized by conscious or unconscious attempt to manipulate other people for acceptance. People who adopt semi-belonging styles often plead, coerce, exploit, cajole, demand, and comply in efforts to belong to other people. Such efforts seldom work. In the final analysis, we cannot make other people love and accept us. But we can increase the probability that other people will want to belong to us and want us to belong to them. Psychologists call it the law of reciprocity. People tend to act toward us in relatively the same way that they perceive that we are acting toward them. Jesus stated it this way, "Therefore, all things whatsoever ye would that men would do to you, do ye even so to them.'' Thus, we set the style for our relationships by the way we act toward people.

The Pursuit of Intimacy

Intimacy is the grasping of the internal world of another person. It is the quality or condition of being close to another person. It is never a unilateral experience. That is, one cannot deliberately become intimate with another person unless the other person desires intimacy. Intimacy is dependent on mutual love and two-way communication between two or more people.

The pursuit of intimacy requires self-awareness. When a person is in touch with himself, he is more conscious of his needs and motivations. The less he is in touch with his inner kingdom, the more likely the possibility that he may seek to manipulate other people for their love and acceptance. The process of getting in touch with self is referred to by one writer as "checking in."

> The magic words of checking in are *how* and *what*. How am I belonging to this person right now? What is the extra message I may be sending? Am I pitifully pouting, burrowing into his heart, and gouging a chunk of compassion for his acceptance of me? Am I coercing him with my stabbing sarcasm to think as I think? Am I belly-laughing at a mediocre joke to extract the approval of the joke teller? Am I being super agreeable to keep him glued to me? Am I straining to find out what he expects of me so that I can comply, thus buying his acceptance of me? Am I displaying how helpless and indecisive I am, milking his help? [3]

Simply stated, checking in is learning to perceive yourself objectively, to "get outside yourself" and see yourself as you think others may see you. Checking in is a skill that can be developed and improved. At first, one may be overwhelmed with the fact that he has been deceiving himself by not checking in previously. He begins to learn more about his own needs, which he has subtly attempted to manipulate other people to fulfill.

A corollary to checking in is checking out. Checking out is the process of receiving feedback from persons with whom we relate. Checking out helps us to see if we are indeed communicating to others what we think we are communicating.

In their book, *Meta-talk,* Nurenberg and Calerno remind us:

> Talk exists on at least three levels of meaning: (1) What the speaker is saying; (2) What the speaker thinks he is saying, and (3) What the listener thinks he is saying. The first level requires little consideration. The second and third levels require much more consideration than the first. Here is where the differences may arise; while the speaker thinks he is being understood on one level, the listener may be listening on an entirely different level.[4]

Checking out may be achieved in two ways. First, there is nonverbal feedback. What do I sense about the way the other person responds to my message? Do I sense anxiety? anger? fear? boredom? joy? acceptance? rejection? The second way is by securing verbal feedback, by asking the other person to state how we are coming across. Such verbal feedback usually will be given if the other person is relatively certain that you will receive it to learn from it.

Intimacy with other people will more likely be achieved if we claim ownership for our thoughts, feelings, and actions. Ownership for our thoughts, feelings, and actions means that

we do not blame others for them. For example, we don't say:
"You frustrate me." We do say, "I am frustrated." The
difference is that we choose to become frustrated by the actions of another person. We might just as easily be pleased if
we so choose. In other words, our responses to other people
are always a matter of choice. Our feelings belong to us.

> Of course, we feel better assigning our emotions to other
> people. You made me angry . . . you made me jealous . . .
> you frightened me . . . The fact is that you can't make me
> anything. You can only stimulate the emotions that are already
> in me, waiting to be activated. The distinction between *causing*
> and *stimulating* the emotion is not just a play on words. If I
> think you can make me angry, I simply lay the blame and pin
> the problem on you. I can then walk away from our encounter
> learning nothing, concluding that you were at fault because
> you made me angry. Then I need to ask no questions of myself
> because I have laid all the responsibility at your feet.[5]

When we blame other people for the way we feel, we may
communicate the idea that "You are responsible for the way I
feel. Therefore, you must be careful not to do anything that
will make me feel bad." Such a relationship is a barrier to
intimacy. People either abandon the relationship or develop a
semi-belonging style that is contrived and superficial in an effort
not to stimulate the negative feeling and then be blamed for
them.

Intimacy with other people is better achieved when we are
willing to be open in our interpersonal relationship. Openness
means sharing with other people the happenings in the inner
kingdom. John Powell in his book, *The Secret of Staying in
Love,* points out two ways to communicate with people. One
way is *discussion,* the act of telling others factual information.

The other type of communication is dialogue. Dialogue sharing feelings, hopes, and dreams—those thoughts and feelings that come from the core of our being. Dialogue is one way we express openness.

Openness is essential to intimacy because intimacy demands knowledge of personhood. We cannot be intimate with people we do not know and people cannot be intimate with us unless we let them know who we are.

Openness requires risk. When we are open with others, when we share our private worlds, we become vulnerable. Others may, if they wish, betray that trust by improperly using the intimate information we have shared. But unless we are willing to take the chance we may not develop close relationships with other people.

The rewards of openness are those of becoming real with other people and discovering that other people are real with us. Through this process we grow. Openness is a life-transforming quality. Margery Williams in the *Velveteen Rabbit* describes the effects of openness in helping us to become real.

"Real isn't how you are made," said the Skin Horse. "It's a thing that happens to you. When a child loves you for a long, long time, not just to play with, but REALLY loves you, then you become Real. It doesn't happen all at once. You become. It takes a long time. Generally, by the time you are Real, most of your hair has been loved off, and your eyes drop out and you get loose in the joints and very shabby. But these things don't matter at all, because once you are Real you can't be ugly, except to people who don't understand." [6]

Empathy is an essential characteristic of intimacy. Empathy is the process of placing oneself in the frame of reference of another, feeling the world as he feels it, sharing his world with him.

Empathy is sometime difficult but seldom impossible. To develop empathy requires that we cast off the cloak of judgment. That is, we do not pass judgment on what we discover when we enter the frame of reference of another person.

> I suggest that each of us has discovered that this kind of understanding is extremely rare. We never receive nor offer it with great frequency. Instead, we offer another type of understanding which is different, such as, "I understand what is wrong with you" or "I understand what makes you that way." These are types of understanding which usually offer and receive—an evaluative understanding from the outside. It is not surprising that we shy away from true understanding. If I am truly open to the way life is experienced by another person—if I can take his world into mine—then I run the risk of seeing life in his way, of being changed myself, and we all resist change.[7]

Thus, the primary requirement for developing empathy is the willingness to change ourselves, if necessary, rather than insisting that the other person change to become like us.

Through empathy we experience the other person's pain, joy, hope, and frustration. We truly understand how he feels. It is the depth of identification with another that was experienced by one of Marc Connelly's characters in *Green Pastures* who, seeing the crucifixion, said, "I guess being God ain't no bed of roses." Such empathy is a hallmark of intimate belonging.

To belong and to know other people belong to us is a river that flows deep and wide within each of us. Psychologists study it. Ministers talk about it. Poets and songwriters muse over it. But the development of it is uniquely the responsibility of each individual. It is a voice that constantly calls us to assess the inner kingdom in regard to how we relate to others.

Skill Exercise

● *Circle Your Relationship*

1. Draw a large circle representing all the people in the world. Then draw a medium-sized circle within the larger circle. Continue by drawing a small circle within the medium-sized circle. These circles may illustrate your relationships with people.

2. What are your feelings about people in general as represented by the largest circle? What "barriers" do you need to overcome in order to fulfill your Christian responsibility as a world citizen?

3. What are your feelings about the people with whom you have casual contact each day as represented by the medium-sized circle? What persons in this circle would you like to know better? What persons in this circle do you have difficulty caring for? Are you fulfilling your Christian responsibility toward them?

4. Who are the people in your intimate world as represented by the small circle? Why do you consider these people to be in this circle? Share with these people your answers.

● *Examine Semi-belonging Styles*

1. This chapter discussed several semi-belonging styles. As you relate to people, listen for instructions of semi-belonging. Remember, semi-belonging is an effort to coerce other people to love us.

2. Examine your own semi-belonging styles. You may do this in two ways. First, check in with yourself. Seek to become more aware of *how* you belong to other people. Second, ask

other people to give you feedback by asking, "When have I tried to coerce you to care for me?"

● *Grow in Your Belonging*

Choose a person whom you know quite well—one who knows you and will "speak the truth in love." Engage in a conversation, using the following questions.

1. Do I own my feelings or blame them on other people?
2. Do I share myself or am I defensive and protective?
3. Do I listen to, understand, and empathize or am I judgmental?
4. What are the characteristics about me that you love the most? the least?

● *Enlarge Your Intimate World*

1. Identify two persons with whom you wish to establish deeper relationships.

2. Begin to relate to these two people using the belonging skills discussed in this chapter.

Evasion of responsibility is a great pastime. We blame televi-sion, drugs, pornography, Dr. Spock, alcohol, the president, lack of old-time religion . . . ad nauseam. To all those we must add heredity and environment. . . .

Roger Lovette
A Faith of Our Own

For every man shall bear his own burden.

Galatians 6:5

4
Responsibility: Blaming or Choosing

One of my professors once described a baby as a frail human being with a raging appetite on one end and a total sense of irresponsibility on the other. At birth, we are dependent on others for our survival. Being responsible for oneself has to be learned. Often it takes a long time. We learn by degrees.

Permit me to share with you a letter to my son.

DEAR MARK,

I had mixed feelings today as you left home to enter college—a mixture of sadness and joy. I began to reminisce a bit. I guess that's natural as parents realize that their children are growing up.

The first words I heard about you were spoken by the nurse who helped the doctor in the delivery room. She came to the waiting room where I, along with other fathers-to-be waited with anxiety and anticipation. "You have a son," she said, "and he has the broadest shoulders of any baby I have ever seen."

Your mother and I knew that those broad shoulders would have to carry a heavy load at times—and we wanted you to be ready. From the start, we tried to be supportive and at the same time allow you to do things for yourself. When you dropped your teddy bear from your crib, instead of picking it up and giving it to you directly, we would put it within your reach and allow you to get it for yourself.

I remember how I laughed when you rode down the hill alone on a bicycle for the first time. We were both frightened and delighted by the fact that you were becoming more independent.

I missed your swimming class graduation, but I shared the joy as your mother told me how proud she was to see you swim across the pool all by yourself. She was so proud to see you becoming independent.

Then there were those years in high school. They were tough at times. When you stayed up until 3 A.M. to finish your English theme, I knew it was hard. Also, I was proud because you had learned to stay with a task until it was finished.

I stood in the garage that day and watched you drive away alone in an automobile for the first time. I smiled and tried to exude confidence, but deep inside I was scared! Were you ready for that responsibility? Thanks for affirming my trust that you were.

Those shoulders are still broad, and along with them you have developed the qualities that accompany people who deserve to be called responsible. With God's help those shoulders can bear the burdens that inevitably come along with life's joys.

Love,

Dad

In the teaching of Jesus, one of the most frequent references is to the steward, the man who must exercise responsibility assigned to him by his master. One of the sharpest rebukes that Jesus ever made was to the steward who did not accept his responsibility (Matt. 25:14-30).

The continuous realization of the kingdom of God within us is a call to responsible living. Each person responds to God and his fellowmen and is accountable for the responses he makes. To grow in the inner kingdom means increasing our ability to respond appropriately to life situations.

Sin is more than rebellion against God. It is also the failure to accept responsibility for one's own selfhood and actions. Take a close look at the first sin in the Garden of Eden. It was not just the sin of rebellion prompted by pride, it was also the sin of irresponsibility, prompted by the attempt to avoid being held accountable.

> Eve shares with Adam the assignment of exercising mastery over all the creatures of the field. Her original misdeed was not eating the forbidden fruit at all. Before she reached for the fruit she had already surrendered her position of power and responsibility over one of the animals, the serpent, and let it tell her what to do. Adam and Eve are the biblical Everyman and Everywoman. Their sin is our sin. We fritter away our destiny by letting some snake tell us what to do.[1]

Thus, sin is not only rebellion against God; it is the failure to be responsible for ourselves and our decisions.

Naturalists often tell of an invisible line at a given altitude above sea level known as the snake line. Above that line there are no snakes. Below that line an unsuspecting child or an unwary adult might fall victim to the deadly venom of the reptile; above, they have freedom to move without peril or danger. Like the mountains, life has a "snake line." To live below it is to be irresponsible; to live above it is to progressively realize the potential of the inner kingdom.

Owning Self

To be responsible is to own oneself. This implies that it is indeed possible and desirable for a person to take control of his life in the midst of the forces around him. To control one's life does not mean that he rebels against God. Rather, it means that he can deliberately give himself to God. He can take up his cross, which is a deliberate act. Such deliberation is difficult, if not impossible, for passive people.

To own oneself is frequently painful. It is no easy task. We, like Adam, want to blame someone else. But to be responsible is to come to the position described by Arthur Miller in *After the Fall*.

> I dreamed I had a child, and even in the dream I saw it was my life—and I ran away. But it always crept on to my lap again, clutched at my clothes. Until I thought, if I could kiss it, whatever in it was my own, perhaps I could sleep—and—I kissed it. I think one must finally take one's life in one's arms— [2]

To be responsible is to take one's life in one's arms and embrace it so that it may grow.

Instead of owning responsibility for our actions, we often are tempted to find someone who will be our "guru." A guru is more than a counselor; he is a life director. A good counselor helps us explore alternatives, leaving the decision about our actions to us. The guru, however, is pleased to listen to our ambiguities and make the decision for us. Finding a guru is not difficult. Many people delight in giving advice at the slightest provocation. Sometimes they are benevolent gurus. Their decisions about our destiny are based on what they consider best for us. However, their benevolence diminishes us because it disallows us the opportunity to make our own decisions. There is another kind of guru who decides for us, based not on what is best for us but what is best for the guru. The results of that guru's decisions not only diminish our personhood, but also cause us to be "used" for someone else's benefit.

The most important things in life are things no one else can teach us. Once we realize this, we stop searching for someone to take responsibility for us, realizing that all people are in the struggle of human existence. We learn to be personally responsible for who we are and for the development of our potential. The call of Jesus to "follow me" becomes a call to be personally responsible for our pilgrimage. Only Christ—no human gurus—can take responsibility for us.

The acceptance of personal responsibility involves a recognition of our limitations and finiteness—something we tend to avoid. We usually want to be known as self-sufficient. In an effort to display self-sufficiency, we tend to blame other people or prevailing circumstances for our miseries and failures.

One blame target is the past. We masterfully rationalize that we are victimized by the way we grew up. We capitalize on feelings of victimization, thus providing us a "reason" for the way we are. History becomes an excuse. In essence, the person who blames past circumstances for the nature of his existence is saying, "I don't want to change."

Another blame target is a close associate—perhaps a husband, a wife, the boss, or a close friend. It is ironic that some people tend to blame the ones who care for them the most for the unfortunate circumstance in which they find themselves.

Eve blamed Adam—and the tendency to blame those who love us is still very much a part of us.

How about blaming society! That's a low risk way of evading responsibility. Like Pontius Pilate, we can wash our hands of all moral, legal, and ethical responsibility blaming our actions on prevailing circumstances. Society is an impersonal blame target. It doesn't resist being blamed because those who hear us blame society usually consider society as someone else other than themselves.

Satan often becomes the blame target for our irresponsibility. How easy it is for us to "write off" moral and ethical responsibility by saying, "The devil made me do it." Satan's forces are real. The influence of evil often prevails. But to "give in" to those forces ultimately will devastate us. The power of God in our lives can be stronger than the forces of evil.

Finally, a convenient blame target is illness. Not all illness, of course, is conjured up. But many times persons make themselves sick to avoid the acceptance of responsibility. The headache, the upset stomach, numerous aches and pains, seem to appear at convenient times as a way of evading responsibility. It is easier to get sick than to admit irresponsibility.

Making Decisions

The big clock in the courthouse tower struck twelve as the foreman of the jury said, "Well, let's take another vote." The results were unchanged from the previous vote: ten, guilty; one, not guilty; and one undecided. It was the person who could not decide that arrested my attention. She was experiencing a great deal of discomfort by being in a situation where she had to decide. Her indecision was not without consequences, however, because the jury finally had to report that they were "hung" on the case. Everyone went home disappointed—the judge, the attorney, and the defendant, because the only decision we were able to make was the decision not to decide. "Not to decide is to decide," wrote Harvey Cox. It is impossible to escape decision-making. We always decide, because even in our lack of responsible decision-making we decide to be irresponsible.

To say that we must make responsible decisions says nothing about what *is* a responsible decision. What are the landmarks of responsible Christian decision-making?

First, there are spiritual criteria. The primary criterion is God's will. "Not my will, but thine be done" is the prime consideration for the Christian.

God does not play games with us about his will. In a sense, we do not seek the will of God. Rather, the will of God is revealed to us. God wants us to know his will. God wants us to follow his will. He freely reveals his will to us.

G. Campbell Morgan has indicated three ways that God reveals himself to us. First, there is the revelation of the written record. The Bible reveals God's will in both explicit and implicit ways. Much of God's will is spelled out in explicit ways in the Bible. For example, adultery, envy, covetousness, and many other sins—both of the flesh and of the spirit—are plainly spelled out. But the Bible does not speak explicitly on every modern concern. Guidance for dealing with such concerns, however, is usually implicit in the spirit and teachings of the Bible.

God frequently reveals himself through life's circumstances. Through his providence, he "moves in marvelous ways his wonders to perform." Often in the midst of those circumstances we are not aware of his providential working. But hindsight is usually blessed with 20-20 vision. As we reflect on the circumstances of the past, we, like the patriarch Jacob, are forced to exclaim, "Surely, the Lord is in this place; and I knew it not" (Gen. 28:16). Through prayer and meditation, however, we can become more sensitive to God's providential leadership.

Finally, God reveals himself to us directly. God is not limited in any way as he reveals his will. The limitations are in our capacities to receive the revelation. When through prayer and meditation, we prepare the inner kingdom to receive the revelation, God speaks directly to us.

The teachings of the Bible provide the criteria for evaluating the validity of the revelation that comes to us directly and through circumstances. If such revelations are inconsistent with biblical teachings, we may be certain that it is not true revelation from God.

Second, responsible Christian decision-making possesses valid psychological criteria. Recent research reveals that the left hemisphere of the brain is rational, dealing with facts. The right hemisphere is intuitive, dealing with feelings and fantasies.[3] Sound decision-making involves the use of both the rational and intuitive aspects of our being. Only as the rational and intuitive aspects of our being are integrated do we "have it together" enough to gain strength of will. Willpower is more than dogged determination. Willpower is the by-product of the integration of the rationality and intuition, thought and feeling.

The intuitive aspects of our being are often neglected while attention is focused in the development of rational powers. A "good" education is frequently described in terms of the amount of factual information one can give evidence of having acquired. Because there has been a neglect of the intuitive part of our being, we frequently do not function as well or as rapidly intuitively as we do rationally. In other words, we tend to process facts faster than we recognize feelings. Consequently, there is usually an "emotional lag" in decision-making. The best reason that can be offered for slow deliberation in decision-making is to provide time for the emotional lag to catch up with our rationality.

The process of responsible decision-making may be diagramed as follows:

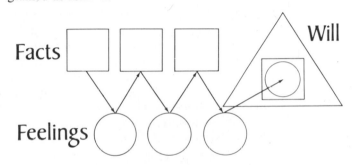

Being Persistent

Yellowstone National Park captures the imagination of thousands of people who visit it each year. Its magnificent mountain peaks and green foliage rest peacefully within the mountain country of Wyoming. Of all the attractions that lure people to this spot of national beauty, Old Faithful, one of the geysers, is perhaps the best known. Old Faithful is not famous because of its size. In fact, numerous other geysers in the park erupt to altitudes higher than that attained by Old Faithful. The thing that makes Old Faithful such a notable attraction is its persistence. For decades Old Faithful has erupted on schedule, gushing streams of water in the air above its cavity in the earth. Because it is persistent and, therefore, predictable, a visitors' center and viewing area have been built around it. One could hardly say that Old Faithful is "responsible" because responsibility is a distinctively human quality, yet its faithfulness and persistence are characteristics of the responsible person.

During the Civil War, the College of William and Mary was severely damaged, resulting in its closure. Later it reopened, but for only a short time. When its doors closed the second time, they remained closed for seven years. But every morning during those barren seven years, President Ewell rang the chapel bells. The campus was abandoned—no students, no faculty. The once beautiful green grass in the lawn became infested with weeds. When it rained, water seeped through the disrepaired roof leaving stains on the once-hallowed walls. But the president still rang the bell. It was his way of keeping alive the hope that one day the historic college would come alive again with intellectual activity. And it did! It was his way of continuing to fulfill his responsibility as president of the college.

Being responsible means not giving up easily. Responsibility in employment means staying with a difficult task until it is accomplished. Responsibility in marriage means working toward solutions to marital problems rather than quickly seeking escape from them through divorce. Responsible parenthood means continuing to guide a child with gentle wisdom and love during periods of stress.

Earning Freedom

Freedom is a much sought after state of being. It exists in

reality only as a person exercises responsibility to claim it. Absolute freedom is an ideal; it is never actual. The degree to which it becomes actual in our lives depends on the extent that we assume responsibility.

The kind of freedom of which I speak refers not to those external forces that may bind us. Rather, I refer to an inner freedom, the courage to choose, to try to alter one's life through deliberate effort.

Freedom is largely a function of choice. The opposite of choice is passivity, a deadening docility that leaves a person in a state to be buffeted about by external forces. When we fail to choose, that is, when we are not deliberate in our actions, we run the risk of becoming pitifully victimized by the pressures and forces around us.

Beyond Responsibility

The reach toward responsibility belongs to all of us. God created us with the freedom to be responsible; we can choose to alter life's circumstances. However, we live within the providence of God, which means that acceptance of those things we cannot change is a significant part of growth.

There are many circumstances we cannot change. They are beyond our control. A measure of our mature faith is the ability to accept such circumstances because "We know that all things work together for good to them that love God, to them who are the called according to his purpose" (Rom. 8:28).

Some people confuse acceptance with apathy, but there is all the difference in the world. Apathy fails to distinguish between what can and what cannot be helped; acceptance makes that distinction. Apathy paralyzes the will-to-action; acceptance frees it by relieving it of impossible burdens.[4]

Often the beginning of wisdom is making the distinction between that for which we should seek to be responsible and that which we accept as beyond our control. The essence of what I mean is given in Reinhold Neibuhr's prayer:

Oh Lord, grant me the strength to change things that need changing, the courage to accept things that cannot be changed, and the wisdom to know the difference.

*   *   *   *   *

The hope of establishing and maintaining a world society based on Christian love and peace can become a reality only as the followers of Christ assume the responsibility inherent in Christ's command, ''Follow me.''

Skill Exercises

Rank the extent to which you agree with the following statements. Allow 5 to represent the greatest degree of agreement and 1 the least degree of agreement. In the space provided, give reason for your answer.

1. Sin is more than rebellion against God. It is also the failure to accept the responsibility for ones own selfhood and actions.

    1   2   3   4   5

_____

_____

_____

2. It is difficult for a passive person to make a deep commitment to God.

      1   2   3   4   5

_____

_____

_____

3. Instead of claiming responsibility, we tend to fix blame on other persons and objects.

      1   2   3   4   5

_____

_____

_____

4. Sound decision-making involves both rationality and intuition.

      1   2   3   4   5

_____

_____

_____

5. Being responsible means not giving up easily.

1   2   3   4   5

_____

_____

_____

Time is what we want most, but what alas! we use worst.

William Penn

What folly to dread the thought of throwing away life at once, and yet have no regard for throwing it away by parcel and piecemeal.

John Howe

So be careful how you act . . . make the most of every opportunity you have for doing good.

Ephesians 5:15, TBL

5
Time:
Priorities and Practices

"The time is fulfilled, and the kingdom of God is at hand" (Mark 1:15). Jesus used these words to announce the kingdom of God. Thus, there has always been a close relationship between the kingdom of God and time. How we manage our time is one of life's greatest resources to aid in the growth of the kingdom of God within. In most books on Christian growth the management of our time has been neglected. Yet time is a precious resource.

There are three kinds of time. All three are gifts from God. The first of these is *chronos* time. *Chronos* time is calendar time, the ticking of the clock, the rising and setting of the sun. It cannot be accumulated like pennies or stockpiled like the winter supply of fireplace wood. It cannot be turned on and off like the television set or replaced like the worn-out family car. In the strict sense one does not manage *chronos* time, for the minute hand is beyond our control. It moves relentlessly on. *Chronos* time passes at a predetermined rate no matter what we do. We cannot manage the clock; we can only manage ourselves with respect to the clock. Thus, the consideration of how we use our time brings us into confrontation with an array of problems related to self-management.

The second kind of time is *kairos* time. In contrast with

chronos or chronological time, *kairos* time is the "right" time; the fullness of time. This is the time Jesus referred to when he said, "The time is fulfilled." This same meaning of time was expressed by Paul when he stated, "When the fulness of time was come, God sent forth his Son (Gal. 4:4). *Kairos* time is providential time that focuses on God's preparation and our response in significant events and circumstances. *Kairos* time is God's movements in marvelous ways to bring about the opportunity for us to respond.

The third kind of time is *experienced* time. *Experienced* time is the way we manage or respond to *chronos* and *kairos* time, the way we perceive time. Sometimes experienced time seems to rush by, especially when time is filled with pleasure. In other circumstances experienced time drags by. Moments seem like hours when waiting for word from the physician who is performing surgery on a loved one.

We cannot change *chronos* time. It is fixed into God's laws of nature. Moreover, we cannot control *kairos* time, we can only be open to God's revelation so that we may be aware of *kairos* moments and respond to them appropriately. We can, however, change to a great extent the nature of our experienced time.

It is the quality of our existence, not the length of it, that gives meaning to the inner kingdom. Therefore, attention to how we experience time is of no little significance.

Human beings . . . live less than the time it takes to blink an eye, if we measure our lives against eternity. . . . I learned a long time ago . . . that a blink of an eye in itself is nothing. But the eye that blinks, that is something. A span of life is nothing. But the man who lives that span, he is something. He can fill that tiny span with meaning, so its quality is immeasurable though its quantity may be insignificant.[1]

Focus on the Dream

In chapter 1, I suggested that the dream each person possesses serves as a frame of reference for the decisions he makes about how he will live. This fact is paramount in any consideration of how we experience time. Quality in experiencing time is a function of the dreams we have for ourselves. The big decision is not "What will I do today?" Rather, it is, "In what direction do I want my life to go?" Once that decision is made, we have a frame of reference for how we experience time each day.

The big decision emerges from our system of values. Perhaps nothing reflects our values so much as how we use our time. If we want to find adequate incentive for changing daily routines, the place to begin is with the examination of our values. I suggest that you review the value clarification exercise at the end of chapter 1 to focus clearly on your dream. Once you have completed that activity, you are in a better position to start using your time wisely.

Determine Priorities

One of the biggest pitfalls in our experiencing of time is the persistent possibility that we may spend our time on seemingly "urgent" activities to the neglect of the important ones. Parkinson's Law, frequently used in business and industry, indicates that work has a way of taking up the amount of time available. I suggest that this is so because of a phenomena called the 80-20 rule, which states that 80 percent of the things we do yield 20 percent of the effect that we want to achieve while 20 percent of the things we do can yield 80 percent of the effect we want to achieve. Alan Larkin in *How to Get Control of Your Time and Your Life,* points out that the 80-20 rule is operative in all areas of life.

80 percent of sales come from 20 percent of customers

80 percent of sick leave is taken by 20 percent of employees

80 percent of dinners repeat 20 percent of recipes

80 percent of dirt is on 20 percent of floor areas that is highly used

80 percent of dollars is spent on 20 percent of the expensive meat and grocery items

80 percent of the washing is done on the 20 percent of the wardrobe that is well-used items

80 percent of TV time is spent on 20 percent of programs most popular with the family

80 percent of reading time is spent on 20 percent of the pages in the newspaper (front page, sport page, editorials, columnists, feature page)

80 percent of telephone calls come from 20 percent of all callers

80 percent of eating out is done at 20 percent of favorite restaurants [2]

What lessons can we learn from the 80-20 rule? First, the normal tendency is for us to spend the greater portion of our time on the 80 percent of activities that yield only 20 percent of the results. Thus, we spend too much time on matters of secondary importance. Second, we can make a deliberate effort to spend 80 percent of our time on matters of primary importance. Thus, we will be able to achieve more of the dream.

Jesus frequently visited the home of Mary and Martha. On one occasion Martha chose to do the "urgent" rather than the important. Mary, on the other hand, "chose the better part," she gave primary attention to the important. For that, she received Jesus' affirmation.

Focusing upon priorities requires that we learn to say no, not only to our own temptation to do the unimportant, but also to the insignificant requests from others. When the requests from other people are not of primary importance, we have a right to say no and not feel guilty about it. Remember that no one else can manage your time quite as effectively as you can, provided you have clarified your goals and determined your priorities. Saying no to undeserved requests for time is not necessarily rejecting someone else. Rather, it is accepting responsibility for using our time as a precious gift from God.

Value Each Day

Every day of life is important, whether it be a mundane Monday or a frantic Friday. When life seems ordinary, it is a good time to remind ourselves that each day is a previous gift from God. It is ours to experience. It will pass, never to return.

Mary Jean Irion stated the significance of the normal day in the following meditation

> Normal Day, let me be aware of the treasure you are. Let me learn from you, love you, savor you, bless you, before you depart.
>
> Let me not pass you by in quest of some rare and perfect tomorrow. Let me hold you while I may, for it will not always be so.
>
> One day I shall dig my fingers into the earth, or bury my face in the pillow, or stretch myself taut, or raise my hands to the sky, and want more than all the world: your return.[3]

Several years ago when I was an editor of a denominational

magazine, an activity appeared instructing members of church groups to clarify their values by writing a brief article on the topic, "If I had only twenty-four hours to live." One lady wrote the following.

If I had only twenty-four hours to live, I'd begin my day at 1:00 in the morning. Being a woman, I'd want my house neat and clean; so, I'd put it in order quickly. I'd try to have everything in its place so that Ed and Vickie and Valerie could find what they needed without my help. You know it is: "Mother, where are my socks?" and, "Honey, what have you done with my hunting jacket?"

I'd also want to provide something good for my family to eat. So, I'd bake a ham, perhaps, and fix the peach cobbler Ed's so crazy about. These preparations wouldn't take very long, for I'd hurry. Every moment is precious, you know. Then, I'd put on a warm robe and go outside and curl up in a chair to watch the sunrise for the last time. I'd marvel at the beauty of the mist that always gathers in the hollow across the road, I'd hear the sleepy twittering of a waking bird, and I'd catch a glimpse of a fading star.

Soon the eastern sky would become a kaleidoscope of color, and the rising sun would drench the countryside in golden splendor and transform the dew upon the grass to glittering diamond drops. And I would find peace and joy in the magnificence of God's handiwork.

But time would be passing; so, I'd slip back into the quiet house and put the coffee on to "perk," the ham and eggs in the skillet, and the toast in the oven. Then I'd wake Ed. We'd eat breakfast as usual; and, before we had finished, Vickie would appear, tousle-headed and drowsy; and Valerie would tumble in, too, all warm and rosy from sleep.

Soon we'd pack a little lunch and go for a picnic in our own special place where years of falling leaves have carpeted the ground so thickly that it feels as if we are walking on a sponge.

While the girls gathered flowers and chased butterflies, I'd thank God for making them strong, for making them able to run and sing, and for giving them a free country in which to live.

But we mustn't tarry long, for the time is getting short. Back home, I'd spend some time alone with Vickie. We'd talk about personal things. I'd caution her to be good and to live a Christian life. I'd tell her how proud I am of her and how much I love her. Then I'd just hold her close.

I'd spend some time alone with Valerie, too; and because she is a baby, we'd play. I'd read her Mother Goose book for the last time, and I'd just love her and hold her, because babies are so sweet.

Perhaps in the afternoon some friends would stop by. Mother and Dad would come, too; and we'd have a quiet, happy time together. I'd spend the remaining time with Ed. We'd talk about the girls, their future, and the good years we'd had together. There would be no tears or regrets. There'd be no time for that. We'd just be quiet and enjoy the comforting presence of each other. As my last minutes drew to a close, he would kiss me tenderly and tell me that he loved me; and our parting words would be, "Until we meet again." [4]

What would you do if you had only twenty-four hours to live? Would you continue your usual life-style—or would some changes be in order?

Seek Time for Silence

Quality in the experience of time is increased as we find time of quietness and meditation. Jesus was a man on a mission. No one was ever possessed by a greater dream or had a greater task. Yet he valued times of quietness. In fact, many of the significant events in his life took place during his times of withdrawal. There were frequent times when he found a solitary place away from the busy activities of people. After his baptism, Jesus went into a desert place to be alone. It was in the silence of a mountain place that he experienced the transfiguration. When facing the agony of the cross, he sought strength through a time of solitude in the garden of Gethsemane. In times of quietness he seemed to have found strength. These times are mentioned frequently enough in the Gospels to leave little question that planned times of solitude was his regular practice. Several references show that these were times of prayer. (Matt. 14:23; Mark 1:35; 6:46; Luke 5:16; 6:12; 9:28; John 6:15).

In teaching his disciples how to pray, Jesus told them to go into a closet and shut the door. It was a way of saying that times of withdrawal for prayer and meditation are essential ingredients in experiencing quality in our daily lives.

We live in the age of future shock. *Future shock* is a term invented by Alvin Toffler to indicate the rapid rate of change that occurs in our world. The future is invading the present at a rate too rapid for us to comfortably adjust to it. We live with an epidemic of "hurry sickness" that places stress on us mentally, emotionally, and physically. Its symptoms are a wide range of physical and emotional illnesses, sometimes leading to death.

Jesus was human as well as God. He experienced the full range of emotions that we experience. He knew the cross was in his future. We can logically surmise that because of his humanity he experienced stress as he faced the cross. The shadow of that cross was always there. Yet in quietness and solitude he found new strength to face it.

Each of us faces stress, which is one of the reasons we need to search for periods of solitude, times when we can let the healing balm of silence provide us the occasion to integrate again our minds and emotions.

> But you see, you are not educated to be alone. Do you ever go for a walk by yourself? It is very important to go out alone, to sit under a tree—not with a book, not with a companion, but by yourself—and observe the falling of a leaf, hear the lapping of the water, the fisherman's song, watch the flight of a bird, and of your own thoughts as they chase each other across the space of your mind. If you are able to be alone—then you will discover extraordinary riches . . . which can never be destroyed.[5]

Our solitude provides God the opportunity to create in us those *kairos* moments when he can speak to reveal his will.

Kill Those Time Wasters

To positively experience time requires discipline. Each of us is vulnerable to time wasters. Becoming aware of them and developing a plan to deal with them is essential to the effective management of time.

One time waster is lack of life planning. As indicated previously, when we do not have a dream of how we want to live, we have no frame of reference for daily decision-making.

A second time waster is lack of priorities. When we fail to determine priorities, we may spend most of our time on matters of lesser importance.

A third time waster is overcommitment. We find ourselves doing more and enjoying it less. That's why it is not always wrong to say no to requests for our time.

A fourth time waster is indecisiveness. Indecisiveness not

only delays action, it also drains us of energy. Both of these effects diminish our will to positive action.

Finally, one of the biggest time wasters is procrastination. Usually we procrastinate on big jobs, thinking that we need a huge chunk of time to do them. However, it only takes a few minutes to start a big job. We can use what Alan Lakein calls the "Swiss cheese" method. We can punch holes in a large job by doing small bits of it as time allows.

* * * * *

Each person has the same amount of time each day. The difference in how we experience that time depends on us. To waste it is folly, because each day that passes is unretrievable; it is gone forever. But wise use of time leads to growth in the inner kingdom as "Time moves with measured steps upon her mission."

Skill Exercises

● *Review Your Dream*

Review the "dream" exercise at the end of chapter 1. If you did not complete the exercise, do it now.

● *Identify Priorities*

Make a list of actions you need to take to start achieving your dream. Use the sheet on the next page. Identify these actions that are priorities by placing an *A* beside them. Place a *B* beside those actions of lesser priority and a *C* by actions of least priority. Those actions labeled *A* probably represent 20 percent of the things you need to do but likely will yield 80 percent of the results you wish to achieve. Spend most of your time on those actions.

things to do
TODAY

DATE _____

		✓	□
1			
2			
3			
4			
5			
6			
7			
8			
9			
10			
11			
12			
13			
14			
15			
16			
17			
18			
19			
20			

● *Seek Times for Silence*

During the next week, seek some quiet time each day for prayer and meditation. Develop the art of silence, of being alone with God.

● *Identify Time Wasters*

Reflect on how you have spent your time during the past week. What are your greatest time wasters? What changes are you willing to make to overcome them?

A new commandment I give to you, that you love one another, even as I have loved you.

John 13:34, NASB [1]

6
Love:
Neighbors, Strangers, Enemies

If you were asked to state one word that best characterizes Christianity, what word would you choose? There are many powerful words associated with the Christian faith. However, the word *love* seems paramount.

If you chose another word, it may be caused by the confusion that is inherent in the word *love*. We use that word quite freely and its impact in describing a Christian virtue is often obscured by its frequent use and various shades of meaning.

When we discover and commit ourselves to what it means to love, it challenges us in no small fashion. In fact, the most challenging call ever issued to people was given by Jesus when he said, "A new commandment I give to you, that you love one another, even as I have loved you" (NASB).

The kingdom of God within us is a kingdom of love; a love not just for those who love us, but strangers and even our enemies.

The Nature of Christian Love

In the Greek language of the New Testament there are three and if one adds dialect, there are four words for love. *Erotic* love is love of passion, emotion, ladened with sex. *Phileo* is a special kind of love, that love we have for friends, brothers, and sisters. *Agape,* the love set forth in the New Testament, is an entirely different kind of love. It is consistent and changeless, not subject to the whims and fancies of passions and emotions. It is a pervading, hospitable spirit.

In the New Testament there was a new concept of love put forth; a kind of love that is not controlled by emotions and passions; a kind of love which crosses all other barriers because our personal feelings have nothing to do with it. This means that God's love is not swayed by anger, passion, feelings, or any other influence but is a steady, caring concern and hospitable spirit toward his creation.

Jesus, when he taught about love, and Paul, when he wrote his famous chapter on love, used the term *agape*. They are talking about our love for God and our fellowman. "For God so *agaped* the world, that he gave his only begotten Son" (John 3:16). "Thou shall *agape* thy neighbor as thyself" (Matt. 22:37-39). "Thou shall *agape* the Lord thy God with all thy heart, and with all thy soul, and with all thy mind. . . . The greatest of these is *agape*" (1 Cor. 13:13).

Anders Nygren in his book *Agape and Eros* points out four distinct characteristics of *agape*, Christian love. First, Christian love is spontaneous and "unmotivated." That is, Christian love does not look for a reason to exist. The Christian's basis for love is not the deserving nature of others. One does not ask, "Does this person deserve my love?" Rather, he loves without such incentive, even as "God commendeth his love toward us, in that while we were yet sinners, Christ died for us" (Rom. 5:8).

Second, Christian love is indifferent to values. It does not extend just to "people like us." Rather, it is given to sinners and enemies, even as Christ loved sinners and prayed for his enemies.

Third, Christian love is creative. When given, it creates within others the power to change. It transforms the receiver. For example, Christ's love for Simon Peter transformed him into a bold apostle.

Finally, Christian love takes the initiative. It is not defensive love. Just as God takes the initiative in love toward us, we take the initiative in loving others.

The Challenge of Love

Christian love is more than a concept to be understood. Christian love, if it is to make a difference in the world, demands action. Love is something we do.

The first challenge of Christian love is for us to extend the circle of relationships that receive our compassion and concern. The Second Commandment in the decalogue explicitly stated that God's people were to love their neighbor as they loved themselves. Jesus affirmed that teaching when he stated the greatest commandments. The Hebrews, however, had greatly restricted the encompassing effect of the word *neighbor*. A neighbor to the Jews was, in most instances, another Jew, preferably one whose ideas and personality characteristics were in close harmony with theirs.

When one Jew inquired of Jesus the meaning of the word *neighbor,* Jesus told the story of the good Samaritan. The essence of the story is that a neighbor is the person who performs deeds of love and mercy toward people in need.

Some of the sharpest criticism ever leveled against Jesus was because he associated with sinners. Here was love in action—love that reached beyond one's own inner circle to encompass the lost and lonely.

How often do we stop to think of the love needed by the lonely people of our world? Are we like the Pharisees who had their inner circle of "neighbors" and neglected people who were lost and lonely? How much I was unaware of such "pockets" of our society was vividly brought to my attention recently. A group of ladies invited me to visit the Tennessee State Prison for Women. I accepted their invitation and went to the prison with most of the usual stereotypes of prison people in my mind. I expected them to be tough and incompassionate. Instead, I found that for the most part they were very tender and compassionate people—people who were lonely and, for the most part, forgotten. Since that visit, I have given a lot of thought and attention to "forgotten" people. They are everywhere—in prisons, homes for the elderly, homes for the handicapped, and on skid row. I think these might be the people with whom Jesus would sit down and eat a meal were he physically present in today's world. It is an indictment of us as Christians if we associate only with our "neighbors" to the neglect of the lonely and desolate people in our community.

Love our neighbor? OK, that's usually not too difficult. Love sinners, the outcast, those wounded by the wayside? Maybe, with more effort, we can do that. Yet Jesus offers us an even greater challenge. He says, "Love your enemies."

There is a saying, "Love your friends and hate your enemies." But I say: Love your enemies! Pray for those who persecute you. In that way you will be acting as true sons of your Father in heaven. For he gives his sunlight to both the evil and the good, and sends rain on the just and on the unjust too. If you love only those who love you, what good is that? Even scoundrels do that much. If you are friendly only to your friends, how are you different from anyone else? Even the heathens do that (Matt. 5:43-45, TLB).[2]

The natural tendency is for us to retaliate against our enemies, but Jesus says that we should love them. Remember that Christian love is unaffected by emotions. Also, love is something that we do as well as feel. The challenge of Christian love is that we maintain a positive attitude toward people who are our enemies. It is a virtue we must constantly learn. To retaliate is a temptation that we must constantly resist.

I share with you a formula to help you love your enemies. It is not a foolproof formula, but when earnestly used can help us resist the urge to retaliate and follow Christ's teachings to love.

First, remember that God loves all people. "He gives the sunlight to both the evil and the good, and sends the rain on the just and the unjust." Because a person differs with you in no way diminishes God's love for him. To think so is the epitome of egocentricity.

Second, be aware that you may not be the target of the other person's hostility. You may be only the occasion for his hostile expressions. When a person is frustrated and lashes out at you in anger, you may not be the target. Sometimes it is true; people are trying to hurt you. But most of the time they are merely venting pent-up frustration, and you happen to be a convenient substitute for the real target.

Third, pray for your enemies. You may not want to. You may not feel like it. But that's the main reason why you should. When you pray for your enemies, you have to forgive them. Jesus taught, "If you do not forgive men their trespasses, neither will your Heavenly Father forgive your trespasses."

Fourth, continue praying and forgiving your enemies until you have worked through any hostility that you feel.

> Then came Peter to him, and said, Lord how oft shall my brother sin against me, and I forgive him? til seven times? Jesus saith unto him, I say not unto thee seven times; but until seventy times seven.

I perceive two meanings from his teachings. First, we should continue to forgive those who continue to offend us. Secondly, real forgiveness, even for only one offense, often requires that we pray and forgive each time hostile feelings associated with the offense surface in our consciousness until that hostility no longer dominates over thoughts and actions.

The Expression of Love

Before the discovery of the New World, Mediterranean countries were inclined to engrave their coins with the Pillars of Hercules with the words underneath, *ne plus ultra,* "there is nothing beyond." After their discovery of the New World, they removed the word *ne,* and their coins read instead, "There is more beyond." All the time, the New World existed; it only needed to be discovered. To discover it demanded imagination and courage.

"There is more beyond" might well be a worthy motto for Christians in their expression of love.

How Christian love is expressed is explicit in Paul's writings. Read 1 Corinthians 13. Note how Christian love affects our daily behavior.

Love is patient (v. 4).

Love is kind (v. 4).

Love is free of jealousy (v. 4).

Love is not boastful or arrogant (v. 5).

Love is not rude, selfish, or unstable (v. 5).

Love rejoices in the right (v. 6).

Love assumes the best about people (v. 7).

Love is enduring (v. 8).

Paul made it clear that Christian love is something which, if absent, makes everything else nothing (vv. 1-3).

Christian love is love that turns the other cheek (see Matt. 5:39), and goes the second mile (see Matt. 5:41). It involves putting away negative, childish actions and feelings. "When I was a child, I spake as a child, . . . I thought as a child: but when I became a man, I put away childish things" (1 Cor. 13:11). The extent of our practice of mature love is a measure of our growth toward maturity. Our quest for continued growth is our ability to express Christian love in an unending fashion.

The lure of love is the power that it provides both to the giver and the receiver. Jesus said, "You shall receive power, after that the Holy Spirit is come upon you (Acts 1:8). That power is realized only as it fills the inner kingdom to motivate and guide us with its gentle wisdom.

Skill Developers

● *Love a Neighbor*

During the next month, be sensitive to the needs of a fellow Christian who may need a special expression of your love. Examples may include the death of a relative, loss of a job, confinement to a hospital, or marital difficulty. Express Christian love by performing an act of helpfulness.

● *Love a Stranger*

Think of the people in your community with whom you

have little or no contact. Seek to get to know some of these people and to express Christian love toward them in some specific manner.

● *Love an Enemy*

Identify a person with whom your association has been negative. Use the formula for loving your enemies described in this chapter as you seek to nourish Christian love toward that person.

But when the Holy Spirit has come upon you, you will receive power to testify about me with great effect . . . to the ends of the earth.

Acts 1:8, TLB

The Kingdom of Heaven can be illustrated by a fisherman—he casts a net into the water and gathers in fish of every kind, valuable and worthless. When the net is full, he drags it up onto the beach and sits down and sorts out the edible ones into crates and throws the others away. That is the way it will be at the end of the world—the angels will come and separate the wicked from the ungodly, casting the wicked into the fire. . . . Do you understand?

Matthew 13:47–51, TLB

Come along with me and I will show you how to fish for the souls of men!

Matthew 4:19, TLB

7
Witnessing: Will and Skill

Those who followed Jesus during his earthly ministry held the mistaken view that he would establish a political kingdom in Israel. In fact, the last question they asked him was "Lord, wilt thou at this time restore again the kingdom to Israel?" (Acts 1:6). His reply was a command, "And ye shall be witnesses unto me . . ." (Acts 1:8). Thus, he emphasized that the kingdom of God comes as those people who have experienced it share with those who have not.

An Act of Will

The beginning of our witnessing efforts is a matter of will. We need to know how to witness, but knowledge without commitment is not sufficient impetus for witnessing. The will to witness is enhanced as we increase our awareness of what it means for people to be lost.

The big jet lifted off the runway, and the city of Dallas was spread out below us in panoramic view. My partner was a soldier who happened to sit beside me when we boarded the plane. Soon after our conversation began, he expressed the joy that accompanies a trip home. Then, he began to talk of Vietnam, his destination after the furlough was over.

"What has the army trained you to do?" I asked.

"I'm a medic," he replied.

As our conversation continued, he talked of the job of a medic in combat. "After the battle," he said, "we go in and treat the wounded men. We try first to help the ones who can recover. If a man is fatally wounded, we leave him and move on to a person whom we can help."

"It must be hard to leave a dying man," I commented.

"In medic training, they tell us never to look into the eyes of a dying man," he explained. "They say that if we do we will never be able to leave him."

Just then the stewardess brought our meal, and our conversation ended. But his words kept ringing in my ears. "Never look into the eyes of a dying man, or you will never be able to leave him." This could be our problem. We never have looked into the eyes of the teeming multitudes of humanity who are dying without Christ.

New Christians usually have a keen sense of awareness of the difference between the person who is lost and the person who is saved. The lost person is without hope. As Paul described the Gentiles who were lost, they are, "Aliens from the commonwealth of Israel, and strangers from the covenants of promise, having no hope, and without God in the world" (Eph. 2:12). The saved person finds in Christ an inner peace, "For he is our peace . . ." (Eph. 2:14).

As we move further away in time from our initial conversion experience, we are prone to forget the extent of the difference it made within us. While we are aware of our salvation and assured of its validity, we tend to forget those feelings of lostness we experienced before we believed. We often lose some of our ability to empathize with the plight of the lost person. Thus, we often lose our sense of urgency in witnessing.

The will to witness can increase as we "check in" on ourselves to become aware of the internal obstacles that prevent us from witnessing. Few of us would deny that we ought to witness. More of us deny those reasons why we do not witness.

One obstacle to witnessing is fear of ridicule. The first century Christians gave evidence to those around them "that they had been with Jesus" (Acts 4:13). They had walked with him along the dusty Palestinian roads. They felt liberation as Jesus spoke his challenging and inspiring words. They were not learned religious leaders; they were ordinary people whom Jesus called to experience abundant life—and experience it they did! Then they felt compelled to share with others who Jesus was and what he could mean to those people who would follow him.

The environment in which Peter and John witnessed boldly was hostile to their witnessing. Only a few weeks earlier, the same hostile sentiment that was present in this group of people had prompted the crucifixion of Jesus. But Peter and John found courage to witness in spite of the hostile threats.

Fortunately, people in the United States are not prohibited from witnessing for Christ. Baptists and other groups alike reap the regards of our Baptist forefathers who worked zealously and wisely to assure a government that preserved the free exercise of religion. We have reason to thank God for their efforts. The believer today, however, is not immune from threats. The persistent threat of ridicule and attempted intimidation is present in our culture. The Christian who takes seriously the task of witnessing for Christ should expect to encounter occasional ridicule and intimidation.

To witness for Christ is sometimes difficult. Often we are tempted to shirk from it because we fear that people will consider us religious fanatics. We feel that to speak to people about matters so personal as their religious beliefs and commitments is undignified. We fear that individuals will consider that we are interfering with their business. In effect, we are timid.

The Christian who finds courage to witness to others for Christ will make the startling discovery that some people will receive the witness gladly. Nevertheless, our motive for witnessing comes not from the fact that people make affirmative responses. Rather, our motive for witnessing is based on the instruction of Jesus who said, ''Ye shall be witnesses unto me'' (Acts. 1:8).

Another obstacle to witnessing is the feeling that we are not worthy enough to be effective. In other words, because we are not perfect, we are vulnerable. We fear that the persons to whom we witness will not accept us as credible persons because we still commit sins.

A Christian life guided by the high ideals of Christ is an authentic goal. We can never be a better witness than we are a person. We will never reach the point, however, when we are not vulnerable because of our imperfection. Our entire earthly pilgrimage will be plagued by the realization that we are sinners—saved by grace, to be sure, but sinners, nevertheless.

How shall we deal with our moral vulnerability? Shall we go around *incognito,* not allowing the world to know we are Christians for fear that we will be attacked at our most vulnerable points? To do so would violate Christ's teachings that as we go, we are to seek to make disciples (see Matt. 28:16-20).

The solution is for Christians to admit that they are not

perfect—that it is because of our sin that we need and appreciate the grace of God. We can share the meaning of that grace with others. When we admit that it is through God's grace and not our own efforts that we are members of God's kingdom, we speak the truth and become less vulnerable in our humanity.

A third obstacle to witnessing is fear that we will not be successful. Such fear often arises out of our lack of skill in witnessing. Such skill, however, comes only as we are willing to risk failure in a witnessing situation. We may be certain that the Holy Spirit is present in a witnessing situation. It is the Holy Spirit that convinces the unbeliever of his need for faith. The Christian witness has only the task of being faithful to the command of Christ to be a witness.

The Practice of Skill

No one ever becomes an effective witness until he is willing to try. But when he tries, the result is usually improved skill in sharing his faith.

Basically, there are three approaches to witnessing. These approaches are not mutually exclusive. That is, in actual witnessing we may use any combination of any three of them. One way to witness is to share your unique story of what God has done and is doing in your life. Often we fail to fully appreciate what God is able to do with our testimony. There are several reasons why the testimony is so effective. First, the testimony is authoritative. When we tell how we experience God in our daily lives, the message is authentic. Second, the testimony is interesting to people because we share a bit of ourselves. Third, the personal testimony is something we all can do. It is a sharing of what we have experienced in our relationship with God. Through practice, we can learn to tell these experiences with the same ease and comfort that we have when we talk about the weather. Give your testimony a contemporary quality. Unfortunately, giving testimonies has tended to be discussions of how we became Christians. While this is often convincing, the person who is not a Christian wants to know how we experience God each day. For example, what are we experiencing in our prayer life? How has the Holy Spirit provided strength in times of trials?

A notable example of the power of personal testimony occurred during the writing of this book. A popular television program featured Corrie ten Boom, author of *The Hiding Place*. She related to the television audience how God gave her strength as she operated an underground movement to protect Jewish people from Nazi extermination during World War II. "When the worst happens to a child of God, the best remains," she asserted. Her testimony deeply affected other persons on the program and, no doubt, many people in the television audience. Each of us has unique experiences with God. These experiences can and should be a part of our personal testimony.

The use of the Bible to explain how a person can become a Christian is a second skill needed in witnessing. The Scriptures were used freely by the early Christians as they proclaimed that Jesus was the Christ. They cited Old Testament promise of the coming of the Savior and indicated how Jesus had fulfilled those promises. Then, they called on their hearers to repent of their sins and to believe in Jesus Christ as their Savior. The Scriptures were used as the authority by which unbelievers were called on to repent and be saved.

The valid use of Bible passages is an effective way to

witness today. The Christian witness need not wait until he feels he has extensive knowledge of the Bible before he begins to use it effectively in Christian witnessing. He can begin with a few well-chosen passages. One approach is illustrated below.

John 10:10.—Jesus came to offer us life filled with meaning. God wants the very best for us. We can find new and greater dimensions in living by following Christ.

Romans 3:23; 6:23.—The sins we have committed keep us from experiencing the abundant life that Jesus came to give us. These consist of sins of the spirit and sins of the flesh.

1 John 1:9—To confess our sins means that we acknowledge them, ask God to forgive us, and commit our lives to him. When we do this, God is faithful (he keeps his promise) and just (he treats us all alike) to forgive (erase, remove) our sins and cleanse us from all unrighteousness (free us from guilt).

John 3:16.—God sent his Son into the world to enable us to have eternal life.

John 1:12.—Persons who receive Jesus as Savior become the sons of God. They inherit the abundant life that Jesus has made possible.

A salesman stood up in a church meeting to give his testimony. "When I look for a good salesman," he said, "I look for a person who not only will tell about the benefits of the product he is selling; I want a person who does not mind asking for the order." Then he explained that the same thing is true about witnessing. "After I have explained how to be saved, I ask for a commitment." After we share the promise of God's Word, the natural and appropriate thing is to ask the person to commit himself to Christ. Many people still are lost because no one has been bold enough to ask them to trust

Christ and to claim his promises.

A third skill needed in witnessing is the ministry-centered witness. The ministry-centered witness involves our performing acts of ministry in an effort to win a hearing for the gospel. Through such acts we demonstrate that we really care for people and, consequently, people listen to us more attentively. When we are willing to perform acts of Christian ministry, we build bridges of communication between ourselves and other people over which the message of salvation may pass.

People Talk

As we become familiar with the words and concepts used by churchgoers, we may fall prey to temptation to use words with which we are familiar but are confusing to nonchurchgoers. In witnessing, ''people talk'' is best.

Jesus used the language of life. This conversation was filled with terms such as salt, meat, light, sons, families, sheep, and sail. One of the most helpful things a person can do in witnessing is to try to translate words which are a part of the church's vocabulary into words which are a part of everyday life and which convey the same meaning.

Frank Laubach spent most of his life helping illiterate adults learn to read. One of his primary methods of working with illiterate adults was called ''Each one teach one.'' The basic idea of the program was that when a person learned to read adequately enough to teach someone else, this proved that he had learned his lesson well.

One of the true tests of a Christian's understanding of his relationship to God is his ability to share his faith with someone else. Like Andrew, who expressed faith in Jesus as Savior, the Christian will come to a better understanding of his faith and grow in Christian grace by sharing his faith with others.

Witnessing is a challenge. The witness is confronted with questions that often demand that he continue his own quest in Christian discipleship. Such growth may not occur if these challenges are not present.

Witnessing helps a person to maintain a vital relationship with Christ. The witness learns that he is effective in winning other people to Christ only as he maintains a vital, growing relationship with God.

The Christian is obligated to grow into the Christian character that God intends that he shall be. The last words written by Peter that are recorded confirm this: "But grow in grace, and in the knowledge of our Lord and Saviour Jesus Christ. To him be the glory both now and for ever. Amen" (2 Pet. 3:18). The Christian never reaches the point in life when he is to cease doing so. Consistent witnessing promotes Christian growth.

Skill Exercises

The following are a list of words heard often in church life. See if you can define these words in terms other than those you are accustomed to using in church. In other words, use those meanings of the words which would fit in the category of the "language of life."

For example, *redeemed* can mean "I am a forgiven person." Can you think of another meaning of the word *redeemed?* Now try these words.

Saved— _____

_____

Compassion— _____

_____

TO POSSESS A DREAM
WITNESSING: WILL AND SKILL

*Witness —*_____

_____

*Born again —*_____

_____

*Sanctified —*_____

_____

*Justified —*_____

_____

*Love —*_____

_____

*Faith —*_____

_____

*Righteousness —*_____

_____

*Reconciled —*_____

_____

*Consecration —*_____

_____

*Repentance —*_____

_____

*Grace —*_____

_____

*Concern —*_____

_____

*Rededication —*_____

_____

*Salvation —*_____

_____

*Sin —*_____

_____

Check in on yourself regarding your willingness to witness. What are the internal obstacles that prevent you from witnessing? What actions can you take to begin to overcome these obstacles?

Discussion Starters

The following suggestions are designed for use as discussion starters in group study. Basically, they are discussion starters based on concepts dealt with in the previous chapters. They are provided for church groups who wish to study this book together.

Chapter 1

Prior to the meeting, complete the skill exercises at the end of the chapter.

● Share with each other the dreams you have clarified for yourself.

● Share the specific goals you have chosen and the reasons for choosing them.

● Share how you feel about disclosing to other people your hopes, dreams, and goals. Are you comfortable doing so? Why or why not?

Chapter 2

Engage in a strength bombardment exercise. Members of the group may focus their attention on one member and state the strengths that the person possesses. Continue this activity until all members of the group have received their list of

119

strengths from the group. In each case, appoint a recorder to make a list of the strengths to be given to each person after the session.

Chapter 3

Discuss the following questions:

- At what times do you feel lonely?
- What semi-belonging styles are you aware of in yourself?
- What does it mean to you to be "real"?

Chapter 4

- How do you respond to the idea that the failure to accept responsibility is sin?
- What does "owning yourself" mean to you?
- What has been the most difficult decision you ever made? What factors contributed to the difficulty?
- Share an experience where your persistence was rewarded.

Chapter 5

- Share what you would do if you had only twenty-four hours to live.
- What do you consider to be your greatest time wasters?
- What are the criteria used to decide how you use your time each day?
- How do you experience time alone?

Chapter 6

- How do you really feel when you are around people who differ greatly from you in life-style and values?
- How do you respond to Jesus' teaching that we should

love our enemies? Do you live by the teaching or merely accept it as a good idea?

Chapter 7

- How many people have you witnessed to in the past month?
- What are the factors that diminish your will to witness?
- Share with the group an experience in prayer that you have had in the past year.
- Share a commitment that you are willing to make as a Christian witness.

Notes

Chapter 1

1. John Powell, *Fully Human, Fully Alive* (Niles, Illinois: Argus Communications, 1976), p. 52.

2. James Morrison, *Masterpiece of Religious Verse* (New York: Harper and Brothers, 1948), p. 278.

3. Richard Shelton, "The Prophets," *The New Yorker Book of Poems* (New York: William Morrow and Company, 1974), p. 575.

4. Elizabeth O'Conner, *Search for Silence* (Waco: Word Publishers, 1976), p. 32.

Chapter 2

1. Robert H. Schuller, *Self-Love: The Dynamic Force of Success* (New York: Pillar Books, 1975), p. 18.

2. David Viscutt, *The Language of Feeling* (New York: Arbor House, 1976), p. 11.

3. Charles B. Hanna, *The Face of the Deep* (Philadelphia: The Westminster Press, 1967), pp. 100-101.

4. Elizabeth O'Conner, *Search for Silence* (Waco: Word Publishers, 1976), p. 45.

5. James Aggrey, "The Parable of the Eagle," Peggy Rutherford, Ed., *African Voices* (New York: The Vanguard Press), pp. 165-66.

Chapter 3

1. Billie Pate, *Touch Life* (Nashville: Broadman Press, 1974),

p. 60.

2. W. W. Broadbent, *How to Be Loved* (Englewood Cliffs: Prentice-Hall, 1976) p. 2.

3. *Ibid.,* pp. 51-52.

4. Gerald I Nierenberg and Henry H. Calerno, *Meta-Talk: Guide to Hidden Meanings in Conversation* (New York: Trident Press, 1974), pp. 16-17.

5. John Powell, *The Secret of Staying in Love* (Niles, Illinois: Argus Communications, 1976), p. 96.

6. Margery Williams, *Velveteen Rabbit* (New York: Avon Books, 1975), pp. 16-17.

7. Carl Rogers, *Person to Person: The Problem of Being Human* (Lafayette, California: Real People Press, 1967), pp. 92, 94.

Chapter 4

1. Harvey Cox, *On Not Leaving It to the Snake* (New York: The Macmillan Company, 1967), p. xiv.

2. Arthur Miller, *After the Fall* (New York: The Viking Press, 1964), p. 22.

3. Robert E. Samples, "Learning with the Whole Brain," *(Human Behavior,* 1975), pp. 16-23.

4. Arthur Gorden, *A Touch of Wonder* (Old Tappan, New Jersey: Fleming H. Revell Co., 1974), p. 82.

Chapter 5

1. Chaim Potuk, *The Chosen* (New York: Simon and Schuster, Inc., 1967), p. 204.

2. Alan Lakein, *How to Get Control of Your Time and Your Life* (New York: Peter H. Wyden, Inc., 1973), p. 71.

3. Mary Jean Irian, *Yes, World: A Mosaic of Meditations* (New York; Richard W. Baron Co., 1970).

4. *Baptist Training Union Magazine* (Nashville: Sunday School Board, Southern Baptist Convention, Nov. 1968), p. 40.

5. J. Krishnamurti, *Think on These Things* (New York: Harper and Row, 1970), p. 89.

Chapter 6

1. From *The New American Standard Bible*. © 1960, 1962, 1963, 1968, 1971, 1972, 1973 The Lockman Foundation, LaHabra, Calif. Used by permission.

2. From *The Living Bible, Paraphrased*. Copyright © 1971 by Tyndale House Publishers, Wheaton, Illinois. All rights reserved. Used by permission.

Appendix

Notes on the Christian Maturity Workshop

As the author conducts conferences throughout the nation, he is frequently asked about the nature and purpose of the Christian maturity workshop. Therefore, it seems appropriate to include some notes on the workshop for those church leaders who wish to know more about it.

The need for the workshop grew out of the conviction of the author that many of the problems and disappointments in life may be attributed to the lack of growth among Christians. Immaturity contributes to church conflict, marital difficulty, and discontent and dissatisfaction in the pilgrimages of Christian people.

The mandate for Christian growth is as forthright as the mandate to make disciples. The call to follow Christ is a call to continuous growth toward the ideal, "Be ye therefore perfect, even as your Father which is in heaven is perfect."

Purposes

The purposes of the workshop are to help persons (1) assess their growth as Christians, (2) set challenging goals for personal growth, and (3) develop realistic strategies for achieving personal growth goals. Structured learning experiences provide occasions for participants to begin working toward these growth goals.

Participants

The workshop is designed for adults. Husbands and wives are preferred since they can support each other in personal growth. However, an individual will not be excluded because of the lack of presence of the spouse.

Suggested Agenda

The agenda for the workshop is adaptable to meet specific needs. However, a typical weekend workshop in a church is as follows:

Friday Evening—3 hours

- Dinner
- "Foundations for Personal Growth."—An illustrated lecture that explores assumptions and sets guidelines for the workshop.
- "Personal Goal Setting."—An audiovisual presentation following structured learning experiences to help participants arrive at worthy and appropriate Christian Growth Goals.
- "Motivation for Growth."—An exploration of levels of Christian Maturity.
- "Exploring My Growth Potential, Part I."—An evaluation instrument is distributed to each participant to be completed and scored by Saturday morning.

Saturday Morning—3 hours

- "Exploring My Growth Potential, Part II."—Group interpretation of the evaluation instrument.
- "Life Skills for Personal Growth."—Lecture and activities on the skills essential for personal Christian growth.